Fanny Crosby

WOMEN OF FAITH SERIES

MEN OF FAITH SERIES

WOMEN AND MEN OF FAITH

OTHER BIOGRAPHIES FROM BETHANY HOUSE

Fanny Crosby

Bonnie C. Harvey

BETHANY HOUSE PUBLISHERS
MINNEAPOLIS, MINNESOTA 55438

Fanny Crosby
Copyright © 1999
Bonnie C. Harvey

Cover illustration by Joe Nordstrom

Library of Congress Catalog Card Number 99–6375

ISBN 0–7642–2166–3

Published by Bethany House Publishers
A Ministry of Bethany Fellowship International
11400 Hampshire Avenue South
Minneapolis, Minnesota 55438
www.bethanyhouse.com

Printed in the United States of America by
Bethany Press International
Minneapolis, Minnesota 55438

Affectionately dedicated to
my daughter,
Cindy,
an earnest admirer of
Aunt Fanny's Gospel hymns.

BONNIE C. HARVEY is a teacher, speaker, film critic, and the author of five books. She has a doctorate in English from Georgia State University and taught several years at the university level. She makes her home in Georgia.

Contents

Introduction

The stooped little woman hurried along the busy Manhattan thoroughfare. Though blind, familiarity with the crowded 1890s streets helped her make her way without incident. As she came to the curb, a kind policeman stepped forward taking her arm, "How're you doing today, Miss Crosby?"

"Oh, just fine and dandy, George. Are your wife and children doing well?" she responded in a surprisingly clear, youthful voice. "It's a lovely day, isn't it?" she added.

"Yes, and thanks for asking," the policeman said as he released her arm on the other side of the street.

An intrigued passerby overhearing the brief dialogue, sidled over to the policeman. "Do you know that woman?" he asked. "She sure walks fast for not being able to see anything."

"Yes. That's Miss Fanny Crosby, the hymn writer." The policeman's pride in knowing her showed in his broad grin.

The other man, dressed warmly for the cool autumn weather, said excitedly with awe in his voice, "She's the one who wrote 'Blessed Assurance,' isn't she?"

"That's right. And a whole lot more. She's amazing.

She walks this way nearly every day. Gets along better than a lot of people with sight. She's still writing hymns for people like you and me."

"I wish I'd known who she was. Several years ago I was really trying to find out how to know the Savior. When I went to a revival meeting, they sang 'Blessed Assurance'—all the verses. After that my doubts were completely gone. I'm so happy now that I know the Savior is mine. I owe Fanny Crosby a great debt for writing that song. Maybe if I come this way another day, I'll have a chance to tell her what she has meant to me."

———

Who was Fanny Crosby, this peculiar-looking little woman with the chirpy voice, out-of-date 1840s dresses, huge cross around her neck, and shiny green eyeglasses? Why was she so well-known and respected by the average person?

Most people today, if they know of her at all, shrug their shoulders and admit the name is vaguely familiar, but they're not sure what she did.

Others, perhaps more knowledgeable in the area of church music history, recognize the name and associate it with some of the old Victorian hymns that were popular in the late 1800s. These individuals often consider many of Crosby's hymns with some disdain. They equate her songs with maudlin Victorian sentimentality and triteness.

But was Fanny Crosby merely a poet of yesteryear—whose verses and hymns would not get a second glance today? What important contribution did she make to the society in which she lived—and to ours?

Fanny Crosby was called the "Queen of Gospel Music" during the latter nineteenth century and early twentieth century. Numerous people, especially other hymn writers, ministers, and evangelical leaders, greatly admired her. George Stebbins, a well-known hymn writer and evangelical singer, gave her all the credit for his own success. Of the blind hymn writer, he declared,

> There is no character in the history of the American Sunday school and evangelistic hymns so outstanding as that of Fanny Crosby, and it is quite as true that more of her hymns than of any other writer of the nineteenth century have found an abiding place in the hearts of Christians the world over. So evident is this that there is a fragrance about her very name that no other has.

Others called her a "saint," and numerous people sought her out to minister to them and to pray for them. During the period of 1870 to 1920, the "gospel song," composed with a simple melody, chorus, and lyrics proclaiming the love of Jesus became a prominent feature of the American evangelical scene. Although Fanny did not start to write hymns until she was in her forties, her gospel songs quickly became well-known, probably because the personal, spiritual quality she brought to her hymns spoke to people's hearts. As Stebbins pointed out, "There was probably no other writer in her day who appealed more to the valid experience of the Christian life or who expressed more sympathetically the deep longings of the human heart than Fanny Crosby."

People all over the world knew and sang Fanny Crosby's songs and derived much comfort and encouragement from them. When Dwight L. Moody and Ira Sankey were on an evangelistic campaign in the British Isles, Sankey left for a brief vacation in Switzerland. To Sankey's astonishment, he heard some peasants singing in German, beneath the window of his inn, Fanny Crosby's "Pass Me Not, O Gentle Savior." Queen Victoria of England and the Prince and Princess of Wales also enjoyed the hymn as a personal favorite. An American visitor to the Arabian Desert in the early 1900s was surprised to hear Bedouins singing "Saved by Grace" in their tents.

Not only was Fanny known for her hymns, she was also revered in America as one of the three outstanding persons in American evangelical religious life in the last quarter of the nineteenth century (the others were D. L. Moody and Ira Sankey). Her ministry as a preacher and lecturer was in great demand, and she worked tirelessly for home missions.

When people knew Fanny was going to speak in a church, they lined up for nearly a block and waited for hours to have the privilege of hearing her. Many venerated her in her later years, considering her a Protestant saint or, more specifically, a Methodist saint. She was sought out by people from all over the world; even when she was at home, people valued her prayers and counsel and nearly made her a "prisoner of the confessional," as they poured out their hearts to her.

She lived to be ninety-five and, beginning at middle age, wrote roughly nine thousand hymns, a record number in the annals of Christian history. She also penned at least a thousand poems and played the harp and organ in concert.

Many ministers and laypeople, including large numbers of women, wrote gospel song lyrics in the 1800s, modeling their poetry after Wesleyan-style verses such as "Jesus, Lover of My Soul." During the time of the 1857–1858 prayer-meeting revival, songbooks were in great demand. Over the next few decades, devotional poetry that had appeared in religious magazines, and lyrics from Sunday school songs, were collected together with the writings of professional hymnists. At that time, Fanny Crosby became known across the country for the thousands of hymns she wrote.

Many of the popular hymns we sing in our churches

today had their origin with Fanny's generation of hymn writers. Prior to that time, hymns were generally formal, rigid, and without emotion. Fanny and her fellow hymn writers tried to perfect hymns written in the common language, instead of stilted speech, and which appealed to worshipers' emotions. Because of what she achieved, Crosby is undoubtedly the forerunner of today's pop hymns and praise choruses.

The story of Fanny Crosby is a remarkable one. Before her renown throughout the English-speaking world as a hymn writer, she achieved fame as a poet, teacher, and musician. And all this she accomplished with an incredible handicap: she was blind from infancy.

1

Early Days

The rural community of Southeast, New York, in Putnam County, could not actually be considered a town. Although it boasted approximately two thousand inhabitants in 1820, many of the houses were far apart, separated by fields. The local people designated Doanesburg—a village with a Presbyterian church, a parsonage, a post office, a school, and a library—as their most prominent town.

Rolling hills covered with thick foliage—oak, pine, maple, and beech trees—made for breathtaking scenery but made farming difficult. Even the rocky soil conspired against the farmer, making it hard to grow any substantial crops. Frequently the men went to work for large landowners, or several members of a family banded together to farm several acres. The humble people who made up the populace of Southeast thought of themselves as "peasants," or rural workingfolk. But the term did not carry the derogatory connotation it has today, and Fanny Crosby sometimes mentioned the "humble peasants" in her rural upbringing.

Many of Southeast's inhabitants were of English descent and claimed the original Massachusetts Bay Colony settlers as their ancestors. They expressed pride in their lineage and in their forebears' accomplishments. The people who settled in this area were nearly all related, their families being made up of clans, with several families existing in each clan. Overall the community consisted of only a few dozen family names. Some clans were very large, but the biggest one of all was the Crosby clan, boasting of eleven families. They lived in a settlement called Gayville because many of the families shared that last name.

The men and women of the Southeast community dressed in familiar Puritan garb. Black was the dominant color for both men's and women's clothing, and most of the men completed their look with a bushy, full beard. The women's black, full-skirted dresses were accented by stiff white collars and cuffs. A row of buttons from neckline to waist softened the somber look.

A Calvinistic brand of Puritanism held sway among these pious Southeast natives. Without reservation, they adhered to Calvinistic tenets such as the sovereignty of the grace of God, divine predestination, election to eternal life, eternal security of the believer, total depravity of the unbeliever, and the supreme authority of Scripture.

Furthermore, most of Southeast's citizens had had some schooling. Little education was required at that time—just enough to read and write—and the community schoolhouse provided what was necessary. Many children found it difficult to attend school for very long: they were needed at home to help with the crops and with the many domestic duties of the time. Nevertheless, having received the fundamentals of learning, the people could enjoy reciting certain classics of English literature such as Bunyan's *Pilgrim's Progress*, Chapman's *Homer*, John Milton's *Paradise Lost*, and, sometimes, the dramas of Shakespeare. Of course, Scripture reading was standard in most homes, and the children learned entire passages from the Bible.

The community of Gayville stood a few miles from Doanesburg. Situated amid woods, streams, and hills, the village's half-dozen houses were surrounded by verdant beauty at every turn. One white clapboard, one-story house in particular dominated a nearby hilltop, and just to the rear of it wildflowers bloomed in the spacious fields warmed by the summer sun. Sylvanus Crosby and his family moved into the house when he returned from fighting in the War of 1812. He had dreamed of making a decent living for his family, but he was already past forty, and the crops produced by the rocky soil seemed to get smaller each year. Proud of his heritage, Sylvanus was a direct descendant of William Brewster, who sailed on the *Mayflower* in 1620 and was a founding father of Plymouth Plantation.

In the eighteenth century one of Brewster's descendants, Patience Freeman, married Eleazer Crosby. After Eleazer had moved to the Cape Cod area of Massachusetts, in 1719, his wife bore a son named Isaac. The family later moved to Southeast, New York. There is no record of how long Eleazer lived, but Patience lived to be more than 103 years old, and until her early eighties made horseback trips alone to visit relatives at Cape Cod.

At the time of the Revolutionary War, Isaac volunteered despite the fact that he was over fifty. As a young man he had married a woman named Mercy Foster, who bore him nineteen children; the youngest child, Sylvanus Crosby, was born while his father was away during the war. Although he didn't win any accolades at war, Isaac was thankful to come home alive. He and other family members who fought in the war relished telling tales about their exploits. Even Fanny later savored recalling some of the stories she'd heard as a child. "When General Warren was killed at Bunker Hill, it was a

Crosby who caught up the flag as it fell from his hands," she wrote a friend.

When Sylvanus turned twenty-one, he married Eunice Paddock. Their marriage produced four children, each six years apart. The eldest daughter, born in 1799, was named Mercy after Sylvanus's mother. Theda was born next, in 1805, then Joseph in 1811, and the baby, Mary, whom people called Polly, was born in 1817.

Sylvanus struggled to feed his family from the little acreage he had, and often they barely had enough to eat. By 1820 Mercy had married a man named John Crosby, quite a bit older than her and perhaps not much younger than her father, who was probably his distant cousin. The couple settled into Mercy's parental home to help out.

Two months before her twenty-first birthday, on March 24, 1820, Mercy gave birth to a baby girl, who was named Frances Jane Crosby after one of her mother's aunts.

In late April, however, the Crosbys became concerned that something was wrong with the baby's eyes. The family tried to get proper medical help for her, but little was available in their area. At last they located a man who called himself a physician. Eighty-six years later, Fanny said that he was a "stranger" whom the family trusted to help in their time of need. But the so-called doctor horrified them all by placing hot poultices on the baby's inflamed eyes and told the parents the treatment would draw the infection out. The infection disappeared, leaving ugly white scars, but as time passed, little Fanny Jane made no response to objects held in front of her face.

The Crosbys, in their great distress, spread the word around the community and the surrounding area that the "doctor" had blinded their baby. Of course, perhaps fearing a tar and feathering, or worse, the man left the community never to return.

Before the year was out, the family suffered another tragedy. In November 1820 John Crosby worked in the fields despite the cold, rainy weather and became badly chilled. The next day he became very ill, and a few days later he died.

Mercy, a widow at twenty-one, realized her father could not possibly support a household of six persons on his meager income. So to alleviate the situation, she took a job as a maidservant for a wealthy neighboring family. Mercy's mother had agreed to take good care of baby Fanny Jane.

Despite their being very poor, the Crosbys' faith enabled them to rejoice in what they had. In the daytime, Eunice and her middle daughter, Theda, did the housework and looked after Fanny, and Polly, who was just three years older. They were more like sisters than niece and aunt. In the evenings when the family gathered by the fireplace, they would read and recite poetry. Fanny Jane, being an impressionable child, listened eagerly to the ballad of "Rinaldo Rhinaldine," the robber chieftain; the tales of Robin Hood; the *Iliad*; the *Odyssey*; *Paradise Lost*; and the Bible.

Grandmother Eunice took a special interest in her little granddaughter, and for Fanny's first four or five years, Eunice was closer to her than her mother. When it seemed likely that Fanny Jane would not regain her sight, Eunice made up her mind to be the little girl's eyes. She decided then and there that Fanny Jane would not go through life as a helpless invalid, dependent on others as most blind people were at that time.

Eunice attempted to describe the physical world to the little girl in terms she hoped she would understand. Many years later, Fanny recalled her grandmother "taking me on her knee and rocking me while she told

me of the beautiful sun with its sunrise and sunset."
Fanny did have some light perception and could often
distinguish various hues, so it is not surprising that Eunice was able to describe colors to her. Fanny also
learned about birds: "One day I heard a strange sound
coming from the meadow, saying, 'Whippoorwill.'
Grandma told me about the bird that gave out that curious note and described its mottled wings and reddish
brown breast and white bristled tail."

In addition, Eunice developed special ways to teach
Fanny. For example, when she used the word "bristled,"
she also placed in her hands a surface corresponding to
the word. Little Fanny absorbed everything, and it was
not long before she knew the color and shape of the birds
that produced different sounds: the meadowlark, the
cuckoo, the song sparrow, the goldfinch, the yellow warbler, the wren, and the robin.

Fanny's incredible grandmother possessed a knack
for instructing her little granddaughter. In fact, though
Eunice lacked much formal education, the teaching and
skill she lavished on Fanny reaped marvelous results in
the child. Not only did Eunice teach her about birds, she
taught her about botany as well. When Fanny was little
more than four years old, the violet became her favorite
flower—and would always be. Eunice and Fanny
walked together in the fall, and as they strolled along
Eunice told her about the different trees and their
leaves. Fanny became acquainted with the trees as she
did the flowers, by means of smell and touch; the leaves
she knew by "handling and remembering." Teacher Eunice realized that Fanny would have to rely on her memory as people who have sight rely on their eyes. She
would "test" her on the things she told her. One day she
gathered a pile of autumn leaves, placed them one at a
time in Fanny's small hands, and asked her, "Now, what
tree is this one from?" Fanny's early training gained her

not only an amazing memory but a wonderful power of description.

Fanny's spiritual progress was also molded by her grandmother. While all the Crosbys were solemn Christians, Eunice had a saintly air about her. As a result, she viewed all the world as God's book and every natural phenomenon as a manifestation of God. Eunice, according to the prevailing thought of the day, viewed nature as a mirror of the spiritual world. For little Fanny Jane, the walks she enjoyed with Grandma over the hills and through the fields were walks with God, as Eunice explained that each tree, each flower, and each bird was designed by God to serve His plan and purpose—that not a sparrow falls to the ground without God seeing it and that God has numbered the hairs on our heads.

Not only did Eunice provide schooling coupled with love for Fanny, but she also became a tremendous strength to her daughter Mercy. The difficulties Mercy faced often seemed overwhelming. She would work all day to support her child, then return at night too weary to spend much time with her. In addition, thoughts assailed Mercy as to what would become of her hopelessly handicapped daughter. How would she manage as she grew older? Sometimes Mercy collapsed on her rough-hewn cot from sheer exhaustion and worry. At those times, Eunice would kneel down beside her, place her work-worn hand on Mercy's thin shoulder, and recite from a favorite hymn or quote the old Puritan adage that had been a favorite of the Puritan leader Cotton Mather: "What can't be cured can be endured." In later life Fanny Crosby would pass on this proverb to all who came to her with their problems.

As far back as Fanny could recall, her grandmother would gather the children and read the Bible to them. Fanny remembered, "The stories of the Holy Book came from her lips and entered my heart and took deep root there." Her grandmother not only read the stories, she took time to explain their meaning in terms the children could understand. While in her old rocking chair, Eunice would remind the children of "a kind heavenly Father who sent His only Son, Jesus Christ, into this world to be the Savior and Friend of all mankind."

In addition to Eunice being a woman of the Bible, she was also "a firm believer in prayer." She knew that prayer held the key to success in the Christian life. She called it not simply a mental exercise, but a close communication with her loving Savior. So Eunice passed on to Fanny her need to call upon God in every circumstance, thanking Him for everything good that happened and telling Him about her problems. Fanny's grandmother told her, too, that there was nothing too difficult for God to do and that whatever the need might be He could take care of it. Even if the request appeared extravagant or unlikely, God would grant it—if it were good for them. If their heavenly Father chose not to grant the request, they should not be downcast, for He would provide something better. Thus they could rejoice and trust God in every circumstance. Because of Eunice's positive outlook, her young grandchild learned to bear the sufferings and frustrations of this life patiently and cheerfully, knowing that God was leading her.

On summer Sundays the Crosby family walked barefoot—like the other villagers—carrying their shoes to church. Upon arrival, they retreated to a nearby horse shed, put their shoes on, freshened up, and entered the church. In wintertime a potbellied stove in the center of the sanctuary heated the wooden building. The stove's heat was hard to regulate, however, which created a stifling atmosphere: sudden blasts of heat and, in the room's corners, pockets of cold. At noon the congregation left for their homes to eat lunch, then returned for the afternoon preaching. A congregational member noted, "As long as they got home in time to milk the cows, they didn't mind."

The Southeast church had no organ, nor did the people sing hymns as such. Like the early Puritans, the theologians of the era did not believe in hymns of human composition; the only music they used consisted of the Psalms, which were "dictated" from God to David. The congregation chanted them in "plainsong" without any musical accompaniment. At times they would use renditions of Isaac Watts' eighteenth-century metrical paraphrases of various psalms.

The only person in the room with a copy of the hymn was a deacon who stood at the "desk" or podium. He would recite one line of the psalm, and the congregation would repeat it after him, until the entire psalm had been chanted.

Even as a small child, Fanny Jane did not care for this lifeless form of church music. She was reserved and thoughtful but always happy. On pleasant days, she walked to a large rock where she sat with her grandmother and listened to the "voices of nature." Nature communicated to the little girl in a language familiar to her soul. For the most part, Fanny had no realization that she was different from other children, except when others said things like "I wish you could see this or that." Then for a brief moment she would ponder what they meant. Her contentment lay, however, in accepting her lot and not dwelling on any supposed limitation to her life.

Fanny greatly enjoyed singing, and by the time she was five, she knew the lyrics of "Hail Columbia, Happy Land," along with ballads like "Fourscore and Ten Old Bachelors."

Eunice and Mercy allowed Fanny and her aunt Polly considerable freedom. Instead of keeping the little girls continually within reach, they were allowed to play in the vicinity of the house. They also let them play outside at night with the other children in town. Of course, playing at night made little difference to Fanny.

2

Childhood Days

Mercy never gave up hope of a cure for her little girl. When Mercy thought she had collected enough money, helped by her neighbors' generous contributions, she and five-year-old Fanny made the trip to Columbia University School of Medicine in New York City. There Mercy hoped her daughter could be examined by Dr. Valentine Mott, one of America's finest surgeons.

For little Fanny, the bumpy, exhausting trip by market wagon to Sing Sing, then by boat to New York City, was a great adventure. She quickly became friends with the boat captain and crew, and soon she clapped her hands over the tall tales the captain told her. But she also enchanted the crew and passengers by singing the little songs she knew. The boat skipper delighted in the little girl's music; he would send for her, telling her he was "blue," and then ask her to sing for him.

By the time they reached New York, however, the trip's joy was short-lived. Mercy and Fanny were escorted to Dr. Mott's office, where an eye specialist had been summoned. Mercy's worst fears were confirmed: the "doctor" who had treated Fanny Jane's eyes as a baby had completely destroyed them. The poultice applications had burned her corneas, causing scar tissue to form and a subsequent lack of vision comparable to looking through a glazed or iced-over window. Fanny could perceive some light and color, but little else. The doctors said they could do nothing to help the little girl; the damage was permanent.

Mercy could scarcely believe the dreaded words. Usually composed and reserved, she burst into tears. For five years she had scrimped and saved in the hope that something could be done to help Fanny regain her sight. Now she had learned the terrible truth.

In spite of the grave diagnosis, Fanny was not completely blind, in the sense that even in her old age she could tell day from night. When a friend commented that she wished Fanny could see the sunlight on a particularly lovely day, Fanny gushed, "I know it. I feel it. And I see it, too!"

During the return boat trip from New York on that spring afternoon in 1825, Fanny Jane had a kind of religious experience.

> As I sat there on the deck amid the glories of the departing day, the low murmur of the waves soothed my soul into a delightful peace. Their music was translated into tones that were like a human voice, and for many years their melody suggested to my imagination the call of Genius as she was struggling to be heard from her prison house in some tiny shell lying perchance on the bottom of the river.

When Mercy and Fanny arrived home, Grandma Crosby reached out to comfort them. She reminded Mercy that if the Lord did not grant a request, then it was best not to have it. She declared further that God had a useful future for His little blind child and that He would provide for her.

A short time later, Mercy had to move to North Salem, six miles south of Gayville, where she assumed a housekeeping position. Since her employer had room for Fanny, Mercy decided she would live with her.

Quakers were the main inhabitants of North Salem, and they spoke what was called "plain language." Five-year-old Fanny absorbed everything around her, and her speech soon began to sound like that of her Quaker neighbors.

Now the little girl encountered a different type of discipline. Gone were Grandma's tender, forgiving ways. Mercy was strict and expected her daughter to behave properly. She did not tolerate foolishness. Before when Fanny Jane was mischievous, her grandma talked to her gently until she became convicted of her fault and was reduced to penitential tears. Mercy, however, used the rod freely, and Fanny was forced to comply with this new type of correction. Fanny later said about her mother, "She was of the generation you *had* to mind."

The pictures of Mercy show her to be a somber-looking pioneer woman. Although thin, she stood erect and composed. She had a long, bony face and hawklike nose. Her eyes were care-worn and intense. Yet despite these seemingly morose characteristics, Mercy possessed a quick wit, and she liked a good time. Her devotion to her daughter's welfare knew no limits, and as she was able, she would supply little Fanny Jane with toys for her pleasure.

Fanny enjoyed playing with the village children of North Salem, and they often played from dawn to dusk. The villagers were surprised to learn that the little blind girl was nearly always a ringleader in mischief. Fanny even became a tomboy, learning to climb trees "with the agility of a squirrel" and ride a horse bareback while clinging to its mane for dear life. Fanny liked to climb the stone walls enclosing the farmers' pastures, and when she tore her dress, she "managed to keep [the torn section] out of Mother's sight until I fancied she would not notice it, which was a rare occurrence indeed."

Eunice kept in frequent touch with Fanny, visiting her several times each week. While Mercy worked at her household duties, Eunice continued Fanny's education. When the child was eight, her grandmother gave her portions of the Bible to memorize.

In time, Fanny came to understand that she was not like other children. To achieve many of her ambitions, she thought she needed the strange and unknown faculty of eyesight. She knew that to be a teacher, musician, or preacher, a person needed to attend school. In her life, however, the road to knowledge and achievement seemed impossibly blocked. It irritated her to hear people say, "Oh, you can't do this, because you're blind, you know" or "You can never go there, because it wouldn't be worthwhile; you couldn't see anything, if you did."

In later years, Fanny believed that blind people can accomplish nearly everything sighted persons can. But for the little blind girl living in an obscure village in New York State, there appeared little hope of ever fulfilling her dreams. At times, Fanny became quiet as she reflected on her plight, then she grew "very blue and depressed." During these times, she would steal away alone, kneel as Grandma had taught her, and ask God whether her blindness was to keep her from being one of His children. She would ask Him, too, "whether, in all His great world, he had not some little place for me." Fanny believed she heard the Lord reply, "Do not be discouraged, little girl. You shall someday be happy and useful, even in your blindness."

God seemed to answer her prayers, and at the age of eight, Fanny composed her first verses:

Oh, what a happy child I am,
Although I cannot see!

I am resolved that in this world
Contented I will be!
How many blessings I enjoy
That other people don't!
So weep or sigh because I'm blind.
I cannot—nor I won't.

Although Fanny lacked the essential "conversion experience" mandatory to the Calvinism of her mother and grandmother, God was part of her life from early childhood. She liked the Quaker meetings at the Society of Friends, the only church in North Salem. Here the speaker would give his message in a singsong style, gasping between phrases as he caught his breath. These meetings were very different from the somber Puritan services at Southeast, and Fanny delighted in them.

A great emphasis in the North Salem church, however, was on an emotional conversion experience. Unless a person had had such an experience, he would fear death. The Quakers stressed man's mortality and the certainty of hell for the unrepentant. Many of the hymns told of careless sinners who were overtaken by sudden death and lost. Even as a young child, these scare tactics were disgusting to Fanny. She felt they hardened sinners in their unbelief rather than bringing them into God's kingdom. Thus in these years her lifelong attitude toward Christian work was formed.

Mercy moved once more when Fanny was almost nine. They now lived in Ridgefield, Connecticut, where Mercy found domestic work. Since Mercy could not live in the same house where she worked, she left Fanny in the care of Mrs. Hawley, the landlady. Fanny Jane retained her pleasant impressions of the North Salem Quakers. She quickly lost the habit of using "thee" and "thou," but later in life she enjoyed wearing the Quaker dress.

In Ridgefield, Mercy and Fanny were again in a

Presbyterian vicinity. They lived on the village green; Mrs. Hawley was a staunch Calvinist, "an old Puritan Presbyterian who took everything in the Sacred Writ as literally as the most orthodox Scotsman could do."

Nevertheless, Mrs. Hawley was not strict and dour as many Puritans seemed to be; she was kind and loved beautiful things. Since Fanny's grandmother was too far away to see her regularly now, Mrs. Hawley picked up where Eunice left off in the young girl's training. The task she gave young Fanny proved formidable: to memorize the entire Bible, giving her a few chapters to learn each week—sometimes as many as five. Each of these chapters would be repeated line by line and drilled into the little girl's mind "precept upon precept."

Fanny's youth and ability to memorize were equal to her task. She mastered Genesis, Exodus, Leviticus, and Numbers, as well as the four Gospels, by the end of the year. After two years, Fanny could recite perfectly not only the entire Pentateuch (the first five books of the Old Testament) and all four Gospels but also many of the Psalms, all of Proverbs, Ruth, and "that greatest of all prose poems, the Song of Solomon."

Fanny's early training carried over into the rest of her life. Once she had memorized the Bible, no one needed to read it to her. Whenever she desired to "read" something in Scripture, it was always readily available.

When Fanny visited her grandmother in Southeast, Eunice was overjoyed with her progress. Fanny also excelled in Bible recitation contests between children and teenagers in Ridgefield. The one who could repeat the most verses would win a Bible, and Fanny nearly always won!

To Mrs. Hawley's credit, she did not limit Fanny's reading to the Bible. She gave her selections from secular works to memorize as well, including the day's popular poems. She also taught her many "practical lessons." Mercy read to Fanny, and Fanny recalled times when her mother recited "with great feeling" Milton's famous sonnet "On His Blindness."

During the New England winters, a singing teacher would visit and teach the young people various songs in a type of school known as the "singing school." One of the selections she taught Fanny and her friends was from the well-known *Handel and Haydn Collection* of Lowell Mason (1792–1872). This selection contained songs and anthems in the style of classical European music. Fanny Jane, who was a member of the choir, remembered singing from this work: "I can still hear some of the sweet voices of my friends reverberating through the old Presbyterian meetinghouse; the tuning fork of the choirmaster as he answered the choir from the pulpit."

About this time, Fanny became friends with a tailor, who was a Methodist, and on occasion she would visit his church. She learned to love the magnificent and lofty hymns of Charles Wesley and Isaac Watts that the Methodists sang.

As Fanny neared adolescence, she had recurring bouts of moodiness and depression. She spent her evenings thinking and "reading" the Scriptures. Though she was happy at times, her handicap began to disturb her more than it had when she was younger. She became more and more competitive with her comrades just "to show the world what a little blind girl could do."

Fanny never entirely outgrew this tendency, and even in her old age she sometimes appeared over-anxious to prove that she could do the same things a sighted person could do.

Around the age of twelve, Fanny felt increasingly alone. She had begun to realize that much knowledge lay outside her realm, and being blind she had no way to attain it. She attended the district schools occasionally, but the schoolmaster had no idea how to instruct the blind, and Fanny would quit in frustration after a few days.

Fanny took one of her frequent trips to Gayville during the time of her depression. Shortly after her arrival, her grandmother sensed that she was very troubled, and one night they talked together. While Eunice sat quietly in her rocker, Fanny poured out her heart to her. Afterward the two knelt beside the old chair and, as Fanny said later, "repeated a petition to the kind Father." Then Eunice left Fanny alone with her thoughts.

Fanny remembered that "the night was beautiful. I crept toward the window, and through the branches of a giant oak that stood just outside, the soft moonlight fell upon my head like the benediction of an angel, while I knelt there and repeated over and over these simple words: 'Dear Lord, please show me how I can learn like other children.'"

Immediately the "weight of anxiety" that had weighed on her heart in recent months "changed to the sweet consciousness that my prayer would be answered in due time." Following that night, Fanny rarely fell into depression. She did occasionally because of the limited opportunities open to her, but she knew in her heart that God was going to provide a way for her to learn like other children.

This prayer for knowledge on that moonlit night turned out to be a legacy from Fanny's grandmother: a short time later she became very ill.

Fanny and her grandmother were together one last time after that. Fanny always remembered that "rosy summer evening" in 1831. Grandma sat in her customary rocker, her voice barely rising above a whisper. "Grandma's going home," she said in a soft voice. She told her frightened grandchild that she would soon be in heaven. Fanny began to sob as if her heart would break. Then in the darkened silence, the dying woman's frail voice asked her only grandchild, "Tell me, my darling, will you meet Grandma in our Father's house on high?"

Fanny could sense Eunice "looking down on me." After another silent moment, the young girl hesitatingly responded, "By the grace of God, I will." A thankful Eunice drew Fanny to her, and they bowed their heads in one last prayer. A short time later, Eunice Crosby was dead, at the age of fifty-three.

Fanny's last meeting with her grandmother would trouble her for many years. Eunice's strict Calvinism required that a person have a definite, dated "conversion." It had been her hope that Fanny would have such an experience and her deathbed words would ultimately bring it about.

After praying with her grandmother the last time, however, Fanny did not feel any different, and at times she continued to be troubled about not having a definite, datable conversion experience.

As Fanny changed into young womanhood, she began to display several obvious talents: She had a high, lovely soprano voice that led to numerous singing opportunities; she learned to play the guitar well and was in demand at social gatherings; she became an accomplished horsewoman; and in addition, her imagination in narrating brought her fame as a storyteller. She enjoyed making up stories of charitable bandits—the kind of robbers, she said later on, that "I have not been fortunate enough to meet in real life."

Fanny's ability to write poetry, however, was her most outstanding talent and added to her reputation. She penned lyrics about every community event imaginable. One time she wrote about a dishonest miller in the community who mixed cornmeal with his flour, part of which said,

> There is a miller in our town,
> How dreadful is his case;
> I fear unless he does repent
> He'll meet with sad disgrace.

Fanny's neighbors raved about the poem and sent it to the editor of the nearest newspaper, the weekly *Herald of Freedom* at Danbury. The paper's editor, Phineas Taylor (P.T.) Barnum, was then in his early twenties and on the threshold of his budding career as a showman. He liked the poem and wanted to print it in its entirety. He also took an interest in Fanny, desiring to promote her as a "blind prodigy." But Mercy intervened and put a stop to Barnum's plan.

Fanny even tried her hand at writing poems about death—a favorite subject of the day. Whenever anyone in the community died, she wrote a poem about the person. Later she was ashamed of these poems and commented, "How glad I am that none of these is preserved."

At this same time, Fanny wrote a poem called "The Moaning of the Wind for the Flowers." Mrs. Hawley was so impressed with it she sent a copy to Sylvanus in Gayville. Sylvanus liked the poem immensely and asked Mrs. Hawley for more poems by his granddaughter. He praised Fanny's works to his friends but never told Fanny because he didn't want to "spoil her and make her proud." He cautioned Mercy not to tell Fanny of his enthusiasm. Fanny never learned until years later how proud her grandfather had been of her.

By the time Mercy and Fanny moved back to North Salem in 1834, Fanny had learned many things. She knew much of the Bible by heart, had received some basic musical training, and had met someone who would mean much to her future. Sylvester Main, one of the children she played with on the green, was three years her senior. Years later, "Vet" Main and his son Hugh's publishing house would print and publish nearly six thousand of Fanny's hymns and be one of the means by which her works became well-known.

3

Institutional Life

The petite young girl confidently tossed her jet black curls over her shoulder. Fanny, at fourteen, was ready for a new adventure. Her intense, vivacious personality made up for her ordinary appearance. In fact, her emotions sometimes overpowered her; she felt everything passionately and could swing suddenly from deep sorrow to intense joy. Whatever she did, whether horseback riding, playing guitar, singing, telling stories, or writing poetry, she did with a wholehearted passion that surprised even her.

Even though the schoolmaster at the district school had more students under his care than he could manage—and certainly had no time to give Fanny the extra attention she needed—the impetuous girl still attempted to attend classes and glean what she could, often to her own despair and discouragement.

This whole situation changed in November 1834, when Fanny's mother read to her a circular about the newly founded New York Institution for the Blind. Fanny's response was one of complete joy and exuberance: "O thank God! He has answered my prayer, just as I knew He would!" Seventy years later Fanny could still recall that day as the happiest of her life.

On the morning of March 3, 1835, Fanny left home for New York City. She could barely get herself dressed that morning in her excitement, and the catch in her throat at the thought of leaving her mother prevented her from eating her breakfast. The stagecoach took Fanny and her companion—a woman from the Institution—to Norwalk, Connecticut, where they would catch a steamer for Manhattan.

When her companion could not get Fanny to converse with her, she said with exasperation, "If you don't want to go to New York, Fanny, we can get out at the next station and take the returning stage home. Your mother is no doubt lonesome for you already."

Though nervous and frightened, Fanny made it plain to the woman that she had no intention of throwing away this golden opportunity to learn like others her age. The decision was made. Later she remarked that if she had returned home that morning, it would have been like casting away a "pearl of great price," for it was not probable that she would ever have been brave enough to start out again for the Institution.

Established four years earlier, the New York Institution for the Blind was funded by state and public contributions. It began with only three students and was only the second such school in the United States, the other being located in Boston. The school's instructors drew support by holding exhibitions of the students' work at churches and schools. This was an eye-opener to the public, as not many at this time thought the blind could be successfully educated.

By 1835 the student enrollment had increased to thirty. With the expansion, instructors were able to lease a private mansion in the country on Manhattan's West Side. The students thought highly of the school superintendent, John Denison Russ, a physician and Yale graduate. He invented a phonetic alphabet and labored to perfect the system of raised characters and maps that Louis Braille had developed in France some years before. Even with his busy schedule, Dr. Russ always found time for each student. He taught Bible classes and read to them from his favorite poet, Lord Byron.

Fanny experienced homesickness immediately upon her arrival at the school. Everything was strange. Nothing was where it should be. She was sitting on her trunk, completely dejected, when the matron of the Institution entered her room.

The Quaker woman embraced Fanny and spoke warmly to her, "Fanny, I guess thee has never been away from home before."

"No, ma'am," Fanny replied bravely. "Please excuse me. I must cry." She wept for some time, until another student was sent to comfort her.

Before long, however, the once formidable Institution became Fanny's "happy home," where for two decades she experienced "the brightest joys I have ever known." Her outgoing personality enabled her to make friends quickly, and her eager mind helped her to master the lessons in English grammar, science, music, history, philosophy, astronomy, and political economy. The material was presented in lecture form, and the students answered detailed questions about what they had heard. Fanny had an unusual capacity for memorization, and to the day of her death she was able to recite the complete text of Brown's *Grammar*.

Fanny loved grammar, philosophy, astronomy, and political science, but struggled with Braille and math. Although she learned to read the Bible, *Pilgrim's Progress*, and Coleridge's "Rime of the Ancient Mariner" in Braille, it was very difficult for her. She could recognize a person by the touch of his or her hand, but felt that playing guitar had callused her fingertips so that they were not sensitive to the raised letters in the Braille alphabet. After leaving the Institution, she seldom used Braille; she preferred to have someone read to her, after which she usually had the material memorized.

Fanny considered mathematics a "great monster." The blind students learned math by counting holes in metal slates. Fanny was satisfied after learning addition and subtraction. Multiplication was much more difficult for her, and she absolutely refused to learn division. Fanny commented, "I have never been a very good 'hater,' even when the best material was provided for the purpose, but I found myself adept at the art of loathing when it came to the science of numbers."

Fanny's creative bent showed itself quickly enough as she continued to write poetry. She would attempt to imitate the leading poets of the day, while her schoolmates worked at imitating *her* poetry. When Fanny was chosen to write the words to a march composed by Anthony Reiff, a sighted music teacher, her spirits soared. The school choir sang the march as the cornerstone was laid for the new school building in 1837.

Her instructors began to view Fanny's talents from another perspective. They believed her poetic success had gone to her head. The new superintendent, Dr. Silas Jones, called her in to his office. Fanny thought he would request her to write another poem for "some distinguished person or event." Instead, Jones came down hard on Fanny, telling her "not to think too much about rhymes and the praises that come from them. Store your mind with useful knowledge and think more of what you can *be* than of how you *appear*."

His words stung like "bombshells in the camp of my self-congratulatory thoughts." Then, through tears, she composed herself, threw her arms around his neck, and kissed his forehead. "You have talked to me as my father would have if he were living. And I thank you for it."

Weeks and months passed, and the quality of Fanny's poetry greatly improved. Before the age of twenty, she found herself the Institution's most promising pupil. Her prowess at piano, organ, and harp was well recognized. In fact, she was considered one of the outstanding harpists in the country.

Having succeeded at most of her studies, Fanny knew it was time to do some other work. She decided she would be a teacher at the Institution. She was not qualified, of course, to be a full instructor, but she could teach subjects and skills to new students.

About this time, Dr. Jones called Fanny to his office again. He informed her that he thought she spent too much time writing poetry to the neglect of her other studies. His real intent was to see if she had genuine talent or if she simply wrote poetry because she enjoyed doing so. As a test, Jones told her she could not write any poetry for three months. If the exercise was simply a hobby, she would be cured. If she was truly a poet, she would not survive this "trial by fire."

Fanny became despondent. She could not do anything and failed her lessons for three months. When called to Dr. Jones's office to explain her actions, she told him that her mind was so filled with poetry that she could not keep her thoughts on her work. Jones relented and agreed to allow her to write poetry if she promised to pay more attention to her lessons.

Shortly after this, George Combe (1778–1858), a Scottish phrenologist, visited the Institution. Phrenology is the study of the shape and texture of the skull for determining character and mental capacity. Combe examined Fanny's head and declared, "Here is a poetess! Give her every advantage. Read the best books to her and teach her to appreciate the best poetry."

Dr. Jones found a poetic composition teacher named Hamilton Murray. He claimed he could not write poetry but could teach it to others. He read long poems to

Fanny and encouraged her to memorize them. He taught her the proper use of rhyme, rhythm, and meter, and told her to imitate the well-known poets.

Fanny learned poetic technique and how to compose rapidly. Because of this discipline, in later years she was able to compose as many as a dozen hymns in a day. She was forever thankful to Mr. Murray for his help and encouragement.

4

Famous Friends

During the time Fanny was becoming the Institution's "most promising student," her mother was starting a new life. Mercy had left North Salem to live with her brother Joseph near Bridgeport. There she met and married, in February 1838, Thomas Morris, a widower with three children. The next year Mercy gave birth to a daughter they named Wilhelmina, but the baby died a short time later. The following year she had another daughter, Julia, or Jule, for short.

In the fall of 1840, Fanny, a fervent Democrat, devoted much time to writing verse directed against the Whig rival General William Henry Harrison. Harrison won the presidential election but died a month after taking office. She decided at that time to put her animosity toward the opposite party aside. Nevertheless, her verses had been noticed and printed in the *New York Herald*, and she had at least one devoted fan—her grandfather Sylvanus. He would walk four miles to town and back every day to buy a newspaper.

As the Institution continued to raise funds by putting their students' work on display, the public was kept abreast of what the blind were capable of learning. The exhibitions consisted of Braille readings in geography, history, arithmetic, and other subjects, as well as singing and recitations. Fanny greatly enjoyed these opportunities, and she sang and played the piano, organ, and harp. The exhibitions often ended with one of her "original poetic addresses." Chock-full of stock poetic diction, the poems did not come from Fanny's soul so much as they were the requests of the Institution's directors to raise monetary support. For the most part, the poems contained little exemplary material, although their form and style were commendable.

Fanny became increasingly known as "The Blind Poetess"; she was also the poet-in-residence, unofficially, of the Institution. Thus her reputation grew as much for what she symbolized as for the poems she wrote.

Something about Fanny's poetry fascinated her listeners. They were touched by certain aspects of the poems—especially Fanny's inherent descriptive powers. She savored reading her poems at more informal gatherings; for these occasions, she chose poems that reflected her innermost thoughts rather than poetry patterned after someone else's verse.

In addition to the exhibitions given outside its walls, the Institution also entertained famous visitors by showing them what the students had learned. Some of the well-known guests were President John Tyler, New York Governor William Henry Seward, and Count Bertrand (1773–1844), Napoleon's old field marshal who had stayed with him in exile on St. Helena. Numerous other greats visited the Institution for the Blind, but Fanny especially delighted in meeting William Cullen Bryant one evening. At the age of forty-nine, Bryant had already written "Thanatopsis" and "To a Waterfowl." When Bryant told Fanny that he knew of her talents, and praised her poetic gifts, Fanny was overwhelmed. Bryant told her she had genuine capabilities and great potential, which tremendously encouraged her.

The Institution continued to send its gifted students on statewide exhibitions. These performances nearly always included Fanny, but she began to grow weary of these spectacles where she was overly scrutinized and patronized. One of the questions always asked was "How long have you been—ah—this way?" People would also ask how the blind managed to get food to their mouths. Fanny snickered to herself, thinking of a ridiculous reply such as, *We tie one end of a string to the table leg and the other to our tongues, then work the food up to our mouths along the string!* After several weeks of touring, answering silly questions, and composing "original poetical addresses" to be read at each stop, Fanny was completely exhausted.

In the autumn, the Institution designated Fanny as a regular instructor. She taught rhetoric, grammar, and Roman and American history. Preparation time for her courses took many hours; then she would stay up until two in the morning writing poetry.

The strenuous hours of course work and composing poetry began to take their toll on Fanny, and the Institution doctor recommended a rest for her. He advised her to stop meeting her classes and to skip a forthcoming visit to Washington, D.C., during which she was to present her poetry before Congress. But Fanny yearned to go to Washington, and the doctor finally consented.

Fanny's anticipation of the trip soon turned to apprehension as she realized the hopes riding on her presentation. The Institutional directors wanted Congress to pass legislation to create institutions for the blind and provide free education to blind children in every state of the Union. They believed Fanny's recital would tug at congressional heartstrings.

Seventeen pupils were slated for the performance before Congress on the evening of January 24, 1844.

When each had finished his or her part in musical performances, grammar, and math, Fanny stepped forward. She recited her thirteen-stanza poem, whereupon the congressmen burst into loud applause. The great noise, sounding like thunder, startled Fanny, but she quickly regained her composure. As an encore, she chose an elegy she had written on the sudden death of Hugh Legare, President Tyler's "lamented secretary of state," who had had a heart attack while laying the cornerstone for the new Bunker Hill monument. When Fanny finished the elegy, the congressmen wept audibly. Legare's sister greeted Fanny outside the chamber door and presented her with a beautiful ring. John Quincy Adams, the ex-president, shook her hand. Despite their emotional wrenching, however, Congress failed to pass the Institution's proposal.

Fanny returned to New York on the verge of collapse and did not meet any of her classes that spring; instead, she prepared a first volume of poetry for publication. By April, *The Blind Girl and Other Poems* was ready to publish. The preface to the 160-page book had been written by Fanny's friend and teacher Hamilton Murray. Murray, somewhat deceitfully, used this opportunity to speak of the poet's "declining health." Part of the book's proceeds would go to the Institution, so Murray felt justified.

Since the publishers wanted a daguerreotype of the author for the front of the book, Fanny had to comply. This early method of photography required that she sit very still for several minutes. Curiously, it is the only likeness known in which Fanny is smiling. She was only 4 feet, 9 inches tall and weighed just 100 pounds, but appeared heavier in the photo—and certainly not in ill-health. Fanny was not physically attractive. She had a rather long face and a small, blunt nose, and her smile revealed a gap between prominent front teeth. At the time of the photograph, she wore dark, rectangular spectacles, and her dark wavy hair was parted in the middle and pulled back into curls that reached her shoulders.

Although the book's sales were modest, Fanny's name became increasingly well-known. People in general still wondered whether the blind could be educated. Of course, Fanny was living proof that they could be, and she was viewed as an example of what the blind could accomplish.

Fanny probably wrote thousands of secular poems, although no one knows the exact number. She wrote poems for every occasion: weddings, anniversaries, birthdays, funerals, church events, national events, and even tea parties. When Fanny left a friend's house, she was likely to speak in rhymed verses as she went out the door. Even in daily conversation, she could not resist the poetic urge to say things like "In the Institution I touched the poetic garment of Mrs. Sigourney, sat long at the feet of Bayard Taylor, slaked my thirsty soul at the living streams of Frances Ridley Havergal, and drank deeply from the chalices of Longfellow, Whittier, Holmes, and Lowell."

Sometimes verses would simply explode from her, as when she remarked after a meal, "Now, just as sure as I'm a sinner, I know I've had a very good dinner."

Fanny contributed regularly to various New York newspaper poetry columns. She also published four books of poetry: *The Blind Girl and Other Poems* (1844), *Monterey and Other Poems* (1851), *A Wreath of Columbia's Flowers* (1858), and *Bells at Evening* (1897).

As with many poets, Fanny's verse varies in quality. The majority of her published poems are weak and without merit. Occasionally Fanny would write something truly remarkable as in this excerpt from "Samson With the Philistines":

His hair had grown. He knew it. But his eyes—
Would they return? Would he again behold
Sun or moon or stars or human face?
O heaven! In all our catalogue of woes
Can there be one that so afflicts the mind
And rends the very fibres of the heart
Like that which comes, when in our riper years,
We lose, and by a single stroke of Thine,
That sense, which of all others, most we prize,
That glorious avenue through which we range
The fields of science, poetry, and art,
And trace Thee in Thy excellence divine
Where Thou hast left Thy Name in living light
On Truth's immortal page, Thy Holy Book?
O to be left at midday in the dark!
To wander on and on in moonless night!
To know the windows of the soul are closed,
And closed till opened in eternity!
They who have felt can tell how deep the gloom,
And only they who in their souls have learned
To walk by faith and lean on God for help,
To such a lot can e'er be reconciled.

Several of Fanny's professional friends considered
her poetry quite good. Henry Adelbert White (1880–
1951), who was also a poet and a university English professor, was one of these. George Henry Sandison (1850–
1900), a literary critic and editor, acknowledged in 1897
that the literary critic could not "discover at once the
full-orbed genius of a poet" in many of Fanny's gospel
hymns. He insisted, however, that Fanny was "naturally a classical poet" who wrote excellent secular verse.

Like the well-known poets of her day, Fanny wrote
in the popular mode. Most of their poetry was undistin-
guished. But the average reader did not expect much
from the poets—if their poetry rendered the desired
emotional effect by treating the familiar themes of
home, motherhood, unrequited love, patriotism, grief,
and death sufficiently, it was enough.

Fanny was content with her role for the time being. Because she was known as "The Blind Poetess," she was expected to draw attention to the Institution and to the plight of the blind. Grateful to the Institution for an excellent education, she did not aspire to more; she would perform as expected and, if need be, sacrifice whatever poetic genius might be inside trying to emerge.

5

Fresh Encounter

Though *The Blind Girl and Other Poems* book sales made Fanny Crosby's name familiar to many New York and New England households, her success did not lead to pride. However, Fanny was nearing exhaustion, and the Institution doctor advised complete rest. She planned to go home for the summer.

Since Fanny's last trip home two years earlier, Mercy had given birth to a baby girl on Christmas Day 1843, whom they named Carolyn; then, in the spring of the next year, Thomas Morris abandoned his family, moving to Illinois to join Joseph Smith, the Mormon "Prophet" of the Church of Jesus Christ of Latter-day Saints. Thomas took two of his children by his first wife with him, leaving the oldest, William, behind. William, at fifteen, did not want to join his father in his adventure and stayed with his stepmother. Thomas spent the rest of his days in Utah as Brigham Young's gardener. Despite this turn of events, Fanny enjoyed being home and returned to New York rested and ready to resume teaching her classes.

That year Fanny met many famous people, including some presidents, one of whom was former president Martin Van Buren, who treated Fanny to dinner. After only a few encounters, she pronounced him "one of my closest friends." When the newly inaugurated James K. Polk visited the Institution, Fanny had the pleasure of meeting him as well.

The year 1848 had been a landmark one for the Institution in terms of distinguished visitors, but another less desirable visitor lurked in its corridors. A dreaded outbreak of cholera had spread around the world through Russia, India, and Persia in 1846. In Persia alone, twenty thousand persons had died, and by the spring of 1849, seventy thousand people were reported dead in England. Americans waited in fear and anxiety.

Helping at the Institution, Fanny and others tried to quiet the frightened residents and assure them that God held the future in His hands. Fanny, in reassuring others, reminded them of what her grandmother had told her, that "the good Friend above who had been so merciful to us thus far would not desert us now; that He would do all things best for us, both in this world and in the next." So they prayed—and waited.

The first appearance of cholera on American shores was in New Orleans in December 1848. It arrived on a passenger ship and infected all the sailing ships, flatboats, and steamers that left the southern port. By May 1849 the deadly plague had broken out in New York.

Mr. Chamberlain, the Institution's superintendent, decided to send all the students home for an early vacation, since the disease was much less severe in country areas than in the heavily populated ones. Some pupils were unable to return to their homes, so Fanny and a few other faculty members stayed on at the Institution "convinced that God would take care of us and that we could be of some help."

Working as a nurse to help Dr. Clements at the Institution, Fanny made "cholera pills," which were made up of two-thirds calomel and one-third opium. But by mid-July five hundred to eight hundred people a week were dying in Manhattan. Later in the month a school one block from the Institution became a cholera hospital. Then ten students from the Institution died.

Feeling increasingly overwhelmed with her work and the deaths so close at hand, Fanny declared, "The horrors of the situation grew upon us day by day." Half a century later she could still hear "the harsh cry of the truckman, 'Bring out your dead!' " As soon as Fanny's patients died, they were usually removed quickly, but she noted, "I remember my fright at sometimes stumbling over coffins in the halls on my way from room to room."

Unable to cope with the terrors of that summer, Fanny was sent to Brooklyn for a three-day rest. She felt that she might be coming down with the disease, so she dosed herself generously with cholera pills and went to bed. By morning, all symptoms had disappeared. When Superintendent Chamberlain learned that his most valued teacher had almost contracted the disease, he insisted she leave at once for Bridgeport, where she remained the rest of the summer.

Upon her return for an abbreviated semester in 1849 and 1850, Fanny was able to convene only a few of her classes. At home in the summer, she had fallen into a deep depression and seemed unable to come out of it. Now it continued to plague her. The depression, in part, was caused by anxiety about her eternal destiny. If she had died from cholera, she asked herself, where would she be now? Would she have been ready to meet her Maker?

The last conversation she'd had with her grandmother weighed heavily upon her. She had never experienced the distinct emotional "conversion experience" required by her grandmother's Calvinism. She also doubted her consecration to God: was she totally dedicated? She had never lost her profound faith in God and His goodness, but she had become increasingly convinced that something was lacking in her life. Perhaps she had taken her success too much to heart. But what was success in the face of death?

That fall she attended revival services at the Methodist Broadway Tabernacle on 30th Street. Because of her background in the austere, cold, Calvinistic Presbyterian church, Fanny rejoiced in the warm and lively Methodist services and in their spirited, cheerful hymn-singing. She had attended their services before—in 1839—at the 18th Street Church. There the devout would gather to sing, pray, "testify," and read Scripture in free-flowing, informal meetings that drew in young people. The leader would frequently call on someone in an impromptu fashion to tell what God had done for him or her. Fanny had played the piano "on the condition that they should not call on me to speak."

A close friend and teacher at the Institution, Theodore Camp, invited Fanny to the revivals at the Broadway Tabernacle. At first she was hesitant; then one night she had a vivid and strange dream: "It seemed that the sky had been cloudy for a number of days, and finally someone came to me and said that Mr. Camp desired to see me at once. I thought I entered the room and found him very ill."

The "dying" man (who lived for another half century) asked if she would meet him in heaven after their deaths.

"Yes, I will," Fanny replied, "God helping me." She had given the same response to her dying grandmother.

In the dream, shortly before he died, Camp warned her, "Remember, you promised a dying man!"

Fanny recalled,

> Then the clouds seemed to roll from my spirit, and
> I awoke from the dream with a start. I could not forget

those words, "Will you meet me in heaven?" and although my friend was perfectly well, I began to consider whether I could really meet him or any other acquaintance in the Better Land, if called to do so.

Answering her own question, Fanny believed she could not meet Camp or her grandmother in heaven as she was now. She had always trusted in God and been deeply religious, but she sensed something lacking in her spiritual life. Perhaps she had prized literary pursuits too highly and allowed these interests to take first place in her life.

Partly because of the dream, Fanny began to attend the revival services with Camp every evening in the autumn of 1850. The services in those days could be very emotional and were interrupted with shouts of "Amen!" and "Hallelujah!" Convulsive sobs, inarticulate cries, and ecstatic outbursts were also frequent in the services. Sometimes frenzied worshipers would leap from their seats and run about or fall on the floor.

As the preacher ended his message, he emphasized the dire results of not responding positively to the sermon. Warnings of hellfire and damnation usually brought prompt results, and those interested in joining the church were urged to come forward and be prayed for. People would then proceed to the front and kneel on the cold, dirty floor for as long as two hours, while deacons and elders placed their palms on the candidates' foreheads and prayed aloud for conversion.

Fanny had returned to the altar twice that fall. Two times she had knelt, while the enthusiastic deacons and elders had furiously prayed for her. Twice the hours went by without her "getting happy."

Finally, on November 20, Fanny, now exasperated with frustration and anxiety, went to the altar for the third time. No other candidates appeared that night, and for hours the deacons and elders prayed but nothing happened. The congregation began singing Isaac Watt's consecration hymn, "Alas, and Did My Savior Bleed?" During the fifth and last verse: "Here, Lord, I give myself away. 'Tis all that I can do," something happened. Suddenly Fanny felt "my very soul was flooded with celestial light." She jumped to her feet, shouting, "Hallelujah! Hallelujah!" She said, "For the first time I realized that I had been trying to hold the world in one hand and the Lord in the other."

Fanny's life up to that time, indeed from early childhood, seems to have been centered on the Lord. But something of great significance happened to her that night, and if the experience she had was not the beginning of her Christian life, it signified a profound deepening of it. It could be called the "baptism of the Holy Spirit," a not uncommon experience in revivals at that time.

From then on, Fanny referred to this as her "November experience"—it was a turning point in her life. Her life did not change dramatically, and the experience did not solve all her problems, but it did mark the beginning of a deeper Christian experience and the beginning of a total dedication of her life to God. Earlier, like many other young people, Fanny had lived in the hope of making a name for herself in the world, of making money, of attaining other worldly goals. Now those desires were gone, replaced by total dedication to God's will.

Many of her hymns and songs reflect this experience. Her hymn "At the Cross," written in 1900, emphasizes her "seeing the light." Another long unpublished poem, "Valley of Silence," written two months before she died, describes the experience in detail:

> I walk down the Valley of Silence,
> Down the dim, voiceless valley alone,
> And I hear not the fall of a footstep
> Around me, save God's and my own;

And the hush of my heart is as holy
As hours when angels have flown.
Long ago I was weary of voices
Whose music my heart could not win,
Long ago I was weary of noises
That fretted my soul with their din;
Long ago I was weary with places,
When I met but the human and sin.
Do you ask what I found in this Valley?
'Tis my trysting place with the Divine,
For I fell at the feet of the Holy,
And above me a voice said, "Be Mine."
And there rose from the depth of my spirit,
The echo, "My heart shall be Thine."
Do you ask how I live in this Valley?
I weep and I dream and I pray;
But my tears are so sweet as the dewdrops
That fall from the roses in May,
And my prayer, like a perfume from censers,
Ascendeth to God night and day.

More than any other of Fanny's writings, the "Valley
of Silence" explains her mystical experience of November 20, 1850.

6

Love Detour

In 1851 Fanny became acquainted with someone who would turn her life in a new direction. George Fredrick Root had taught music at the Institution. One day he was playing the piano, while Fanny listened. He was deeply moved by the strains of an original composition, when Fanny blurted out, "Oh, why don't you publish that, Mr. Root?"

Turning around to look at her with his penetrating eyes, Root exclaimed, "Why, I have no words for it."

"Oh, I can think of words. Your melody says,

O come to the greenwood, where nature is smiling,
Come to the greenwood, so lovely and gay,
There will soft music, thy spirit beguiling,
Tenderly carol thy sadness away."

Root exclaimed enthusiastically, "I can use you! I need someone to supply words for the songs that I write. Would you be willing to do that?"

Fanny could not work for him until the following summer; but then she wrote several songs, and Root composed the music. Two numbers became quite popular: "Fare Thee Well, Kitty Dear" and "The Hazel Dell." Both of these tunes suited the trite sentimentality of the era.

That fall Root started work on a composition that Fanny later called "the first American cantata." He would tell Fanny what he wanted certain characters to say, hum some of the melody for her so she could grasp the meter and rhyme, and the next day she would present him with the words. In fact, Fanny would usually submit three or four possible poems for him to choose from. The cantata, "The Flower Queen," became popular over a wide region. But no one knew that Fanny Crosby had composed the words. Root took all of the credit. He paid her at the outset for her submissions and that was all. Some of their subsequent songs became hits, too, but Fanny never realized any royalties from them.

During the time that Fanny wrote hit songs for Root, she got reacquainted with someone she had met many years earlier. She commented later, "Some people seem to forget that blind girls have just as great a faculty for loving and do love just as much and just as truly as those who have their sight."

She was still a spinster at thirty-five, but Fanny's heart "was hungry for love." In 1855 the Institution hired a new teacher, Alexander Van Alstine, whom Fanny had met as a boy during a tour at Oswego, New York. He had studied a few years at the Institution and had become a brilliant pupil—so much so that he had been accepted into a regular college. He majored in music, but he also mastered Greek, Latin, philosophy, and theology.

For some time Fanny and Van enjoyed a platonic relationship based on their mutual interest in music and poetry: he became interested in her poetry, and she in his music. As she said, "Thus we soon grew to be very much concerned for each other."

When Van left the Institution in the fall of 1857, Fanny wanted to follow him. Not only had she had some run-ins with the current superintendent of the Institution and disapproved of some of the new happenings there, she was also in love.

Thus Fanny ended her long relationship with the Institution on March 2, 1858, determined to join Van in a new life. They were married on March 5, 1858, in the little town of Maspeth, New York. The bride was thirty-eight, and Van was twenty-seven.

Fanny's life changed completely. She was no longer the center of attention; now she took a backseat to her husband. In fact, she lived on Long Island, far away from the cultural center of New York. And she had become a housewife, married to a struggling music teacher. The two lived in rented rooms in a country town where few of the farmers, merchants, or laborers had any idea their blind, dwarf-like neighbor was a nationally known poet.

For a while Fanny was happy with her new life away from the acclaim and the crowds. She liked living back in the country, and she relished pleasing her husband. From his pictures, Van appears to have been a handsome man, slender, having fine features, and clean-shaven. He was jovial and easygoing. To support Fanny and himself, he served as a paid organist in several nearby churches.

About 1859 Fanny became a mother, but the child died in infancy. This event was probably the greatest tragedy she suffered in her life. It is unknown whether the child was a boy or girl, or the cause of death. Fanny rarely mentioned it in later years.

After the death of her child, Fanny's country life was not the same. She had a longing now to be back in familiar surroundings. So she and Van moved back to Manhattan in 1860 and roomed a few blocks from the Institution. The New York City to which they returned was a city caught up in a religious revival.

7

Life's Purpose

The revival had begun before Fanny left the Institution, but it had grown by leaps and bounds since then. Two or three previous revivals had occurred in American history, beginning with the First Great Awakening in the 1740s. The present revival fires, fed by an economic depression, became known as the Second Great Awakening and would sweep the nation.

Two human elements that encouraged the revival were the Sunday school movement and the growth of mission societies. The Sunday schools had originated to educate working-class people who were free to learn on Sundays. The mission societies not only propagated religion but also stood for abolishing evils such as slavery, liquor, and tobacco. During the 1840s and 1850s, home mission societies experienced tremendous growth as they sought to spread the Gospel among the cities' unchurched people.

In 1857 revivals began to occur in New York and in other parts of the country. Prayer meetings sprang up all over the New York area with numerous conversions being professed each day. The revivals were so widespread that the newspapers reported on them daily. In fact, the number of conversions was staggering, according to the reports. Over fifty thousand conversions occurred each week in the nation, and at least ten thousand people united with a church for the first time.

Christians went door-to-door witnessing to people in dingy attics and filthy basements as well as in elegant parlors and magnificent drawing rooms. They invited these people to come to Sunday school and inquirers' classes—and the people responded, packing out the churches. Each day over twelve hundred people crowded the John Street Methodist Church for noonday prayer meetings.

Soon Fanny's life was caught up in the revivals as she began attending the John Street Church and became a participant in the sewing societies, knitting garments for the poor. She also attended prayer meetings there and at Henry Ward Beecher's Plymouth Congregational Church. In time Henry Ward Beecher became a good friend of Fanny's.

Another of the churches Fanny attended was the Dutch Reformed Church on 23rd Street. She quickly got to know the pastor, the Reverend Peter Stryker, who asked her to write a New Year's Eve hymn, which she was happy to do. Then he mentioned that his friend William Bradbury needed someone to compose lyrics for his melodies. He suggested that Fanny see him soon, so Fanny said she would.

Along with the Second Great Awakening came great changes in American hymnody. A different type of hymn was needed to fit in with the new approach to Gospel presentation. The reaction was largely against Lowell Mason's theories about church music. Mason, considered the father of American church music, had said in his "canons," first set forth in his Church Psalmody in 1831, that "the sentiments and imagery should be grave, dignified." Also "whatever is unscriptural, groveling, light, or fanciful, should be avoided" because it tended to "check the flow of the soul." Mason asserted, too, that "familiar and fondling epithets or forms of expression applied to either person of the Godhead should be avoided, as bringing with them associations highly unfavorable to pure devotional feeling."

Mason believed in emphasizing sin and hell as well. Any hymn that made the worshipers "feel good" should be abandoned; instead, a hymn needed to be useful to bring a sinner to repentance.

These hymns that stressed retribution for the sinner were now becoming unpopular. People who got "revived" in the 1850s and 1860s desired hymns that were more personal, light, and less formal. Hymns that already fit this description were "My Faith Looks Up to Thee" by Ray Palmer; "Nearer, My God, to Thee" by Sarah Flower Adams; "Just as I Am, Without One Plea" by Charlotte Elliott; "Abide With Me" by Reverend Francis Lyte; "Jesus, Lover of My Soul" by Charles Wesley; and "Rock of Ages" by Augustus Toplady.

Some musicians had risen to the challenge for new hymns. George Root had written Sunday school music, and Robert Lowry, a Baptist minister, did also, including an all-time favorite: "Shall We Gather at the River?" But clearly the most acclaimed hymn writer was William Bradbury. He had earlier collaborated with Root and Fanny on a cantata called "Daniel." Born in Maine in 1816, Bradbury had studied music with Lowell Mason. Earlier in his career he had worked at introducing the organ to American churchgoers. Bradbury's music was characterized by its "easy, natural flow," and his harmonies by their simplicity. While highbrow critics panned his music, the masses loved it.

Bradbury's desire was to provide light, melodic settings for existing hymns, but he also wanted to set newly written poems to music. He found most of the verse submitted to him distasteful and unsatisfactory. When his minister friend Stryker told Bradbury in January 1864 that he would soon meet a lady who could solve his poetical dilemma, he was overjoyed.

Fanny was excited, too. She sensed that God had given her a new purpose. Her talent, she believed, was to be used in writing hymns.

The prearranged meeting between Fanny and Bradbury took place on February 2 at the Ponton Hotel on Broome Street. Although Fanny could not see Bradbury, she was struck by his character. Not only did Fanny occasionally experience visions and trances, she also had an uncanny ability to read a person's character from the emanating "overtones." She took an immediate liking to him. The bond was mutual, and their relationship was quickly put on a first-name basis.

"Fanny," Bradbury began, "I thank God that we have at last met, for I think you can write hymns, and I have wished for a long time to have a talk with you."

Then Bradbury introduced Fanny to his assistant, her old friend from Ridgefield, Sylvester Main. He had come to New York many years earlier to start a music school. He attended the Norfolk Street Methodist Church and was a well-known soloist in New York churches.

Bradbury gave Fanny an assignment to test her abilities and told her to return in a week. Fanny recalled that day with joy: "It now seemed to me that the great work of my life had really begun." Just three days later she returned with a three-stanza poem that began:

> We are going, we are going
> To a home beyond the skies,
> Where the fields are robed in beauty
> And the sunlight never dies.
> Where the fount of joy is flowing
> In the valley green and fair.

We shall dwell in love together,
There shall be no parting there.

Bradbury was amazed. The hymn contained everything he looked for in a verse. It was light and informal, reasonably good poetry, and charged with warmth and emotional power. He decided to use "We Are Going" in a new hymnal due for publication.

The following week he sent for Fanny telling her he needed a war song, since he published secular music as well as sacred. For the first line, he suggested, "There's a sound among the mulberry trees." But Fanny changed it to "There's a sound among the forest trees." Afterward he played a melody for which she was to write verse. Although difficult, after hearing it two or three times, Fanny counted the measure and produced suitable words.

Again, Bradbury couldn't believe it. He had deliberately given her a difficult melody to test her, never dreaming she could put words to the music. She had passed his test with flying colors.

"Fanny," he told her, "I'm surprised! And while I have a publishing house, you will always have work."

So Fanny began to work for William B. Bradbury and Company.

8

New Direction

Two other women already wrote poetry for Bradbury, so Fanny would work with them. Bradbury and his associates produced hymns for Sunday school hymn books, and in 1864 his hymnal *The Golden Censer* contained Fanny's hymn "We Are Going"—although the name had been changed to "Our Bright Home Above." Another of Fanny's hymns appearing in the hymnal was "There's a Cry From Macedonia." Fanny may have had other hymns in the book, but like Root, Bradbury did not always credit his authors.

Most of Fanny's hymns appeared under the name "Miss Fanny J. Crosby." Her husband had realized when they married that Fanny had a career and reputation of her own; thus, he urged her to retain her own name and not subordinate her career to his. Fanny called herself by different names: "Mrs. Crosby" and "Madam Crosby." In writing her married name for legal reasons, she signed it "Van Alstine."

The following year (1865), Bradbury was compiling another hymnal and asked Fanny to provide the words. The music generally came first, and he would give Fanny a tune for which she was to write verse. Sometimes he would give her the title and subject, too, but more often than not, if the verse preceded the music, Fanny chose the topic as well.

Fanny received her inspiration from different sources. For example, one afternoon she, Bradbury, Vet (Sylvester) Main, and a prominent musician named Philip Phillips were "discussing various things," and Phillips glanced at his watch and realized it was time to leave. "Good-night," he said, "until we meet in the morning."

After he had left, Fanny said to Bradbury, "If I write a hymn for that subject, will you compose the music?" Bradbury was only too happy to comply, and Fanny wrote the following verse for a funeral hymn:

> Good-night! Good-night!
> 'Till we meet in the morning,
> Far above this fleeting shore;
> To endless joy in a moment's awaking,
> There we'll sleep no more.

Actually, Robert Lowry, composer of "Shall We Gather at the River?" wrote the music for the poem.

The first time Bradbury and Fanny met, he told her he had but a short time to live because of a debilitating illness. By April 1866 he left for the South in hopes of regaining his health, and he stayed for the entire summer.

Even with Bradbury away, Fanny stayed busy. She went to work daily so she could prepare poems and receive melodies for the next volume of hymns. Other writers and publishers of church music had also noticed her talents. Phoebe Palmer Knapp was one of these publishers, but she was much more than that. Phoebe was married to Joseph Fairchild Knapp, who later founded the Metropolitan Life Insurance Company. Her concept of Christianity involved helping the poor and fostering social reform.

Although much concerned with aiding the poor, Phoebe still enjoyed her life as a rich woman. Her dress reflected lavish, good taste, and she delighted in wearing elaborate gowns and diamond tiaras. The Knapp mansion, her home in Brooklyn, had become a New York institution where she held a European-style salon. Phoebe entertained some of the most well-known people of the day: most Republican presidents, Union generals, and Methodist Bishops had been entertained at the mansion.

Moreover, all of New York City knew of Phoebe's evening musicales, and the music room contained one of the finest collections of musical instruments in the country. Well-known artists and performers came from all over to participate in the mansion festivities. When Fanny and Phoebe first met, they were immediately drawn to each other, and before long Fanny became a frequent visitor at the Knapp mansion. Not only was Fanny able to enjoy the opportunity of free access to the music room, but she also had the privilege of meeting many of the famous people who visited there. At the mansion she was introduced to Presidents Grant, Hayes, Garfield, McKinley, and Teddy Roosevelt. Some of the other frequent guests with whom Fanny spoke often were Henry Ward Beecher and his sister, Harriet Beecher Stowe.

Phoebe wanted to help Fanny financially, but Fanny refused. She lived in near poverty, with much of whatever she earned going to the poor. But Fanny was pleased with her relationship to Phoebe and supplied her with poems as she could. Phoebe would pass them on to a brother who owned a publishing company.

Another musician who knew of Fanny's ability was the aforementioned Philip Phillips. Fourteen years younger than Fanny, Phillips had gained nationwide renown through his song services. He had called on Fanny infrequently to supply a hymn or two for his evangelistic services. But in 1866 he was compiling a hymnal entitled *The Singing Pilgrim*, or *Pilgrim's Progress, Illustrated in Song for the Sabbath School and Family*. Phillips had taken the hymnal's theme from *Pilgrim's Progress*. He sought Fanny to write hymns based on the ideas in certain selections of the book; he would supply the tunes himself.

To begin, he selected seventy-five quotations of a few lines each and gave them to Fanny. Fanny, in turn, memorized the quotations and chose forty she thought best for hymns. Then she composed forty poems in her head. When she finished the last one, she dictated them one after the other to her secretary at Bradbury's office.

Everyone in the office, including Phillips, was astounded at her extraordinary memory, but Fanny shrugged it off, saying that each person without sight has to develop his memory. She reminded them that other people could do the same thing, if they wanted to, and especially if they were not privileged to refer to the written word.

The forty hymns Fanny wrote for Phillips made up the bulk of *The Singing Pilgrim*. The book enjoyed a wide circulation and became quite popular. But once more, few people knew who wrote the popular verses because Phillips, as Root before him, paid Fanny a dollar or two for her work and proceeded to publish the hymns under his own name.

Fanny and her husband had an unusual marriage relationship in that each pursued his or her own interests without getting involved in the other's pursuits. Van had his own circle of friends and activities, and Fanny had hers. Both Fanny and Van liked this arrangement.

When Bradbury came back from his extended southern stay, his health had greatly improved. The following year he published a new hymnal called *Fresh Laurels*.

The title hymn plus ten others had been attributed to Fanny, although some of the names were pseudonyms for her. Each of these hymns demonstrated simplicity, directness, emotional power, and a relationship to daily life—each quality becoming a trademark of Fanny.

Fanny identified with the poor and chose to live with them in run-down apartments in New York City. In 1867 she and Van lived on Varick Street on the Lower West Side in half of a third-floor apartment (actually, an attic). The apartment had no outside ventilation and no running water, nor did any of the other apartments. Fanny and her husband could have afforded a much nicer place to live, but she insisted on giving away all she received apart from basic living expenses. Fanny believed God had called her to live with the poor and be one of them—part of her mission in life was to them. The good things in life passed these people by, and they had little hope of a better life. Fanny also wrote some of her hymns with the poor in mind.

She said she wrote for the wretched souls who "seemed drunk half the time" and had to sleep on the rooftops in summer because of the stifling heat; and other people at the bottom of the social ladder. The places where these people lived were unbelievably filthy and dilapidated; further, they qualified for nothing better than to collect rags, bones, and pieces of coal that fell from passing wagons. Fanny's compassion for the poor did not mean that she disliked the rich. She composed verses for them as well—usually urging them to some kind of social action:

> When cheerful we meet in our pleasant home,
> And the song of joy is swelling,
> Do we pause to think of the tears that flow
> In sorrow's lonely dwelling?

Some critics of Fanny's verse point out the utter simplicity of much of it. But they claim the simple rhymes and thought represent the depth of her intellect. Her goal was never to impress literary critics or college professors; she only wanted her poetry to be understood by common people.

For her own listening, Fanny appreciated lofty music like Beethoven, Chopin, and Mendelssohn, no doubt because she was a fine musician in her own right. She understood, however, that many people didn't care for classical music. The congregational hymns she wrote were for the untrained singer; she thought every worshiper should be able to take part in singing the hymns. They should not be the exclusive province of trained musicians.

In November 1867 a man came to New York who would be Fanny's closest collaborator and who would write the music for most of her successful hymns. He was William Howard Doane from Cincinnati, a wealthy manufacturer. Doane had inherited his father's cotton goods company and had made it very successful. His second vocation was music. During his early years in business, Doane had led church choirs and participated in various musical societies. He also had a fine singing voice and had become well-known in Cincinnati as a church soloist.

Until he was thirty, Doane considered music a hobby. But when he nearly died from a heart attack, he believed God had spoken to him and that he had been chastened by his illness. Afterward Doane believed God wanted him to spend more time writing sacred melodies. A short time later he compiled three books of hymns: the first, *Sabbath School Gems*; the second, *The Sunbeam* in 1864; and the third, *The Silver Spray* in 1867.

But Doane was not happy with his hymns. He thought they lacked suitable words. Even as Bradbury, he had tried to write his own lyrics, finally conceding that he was not a poet, and the poets he hired could do no better.

When Doane came to New York in November, he visited a friend, Reverend W. C. Van Meter, who directed the Five Points Mission. Van Meter needed a hymn to commemorate the founding of the mission, so he asked Doane to write one. Doane agreed but asked his friend if he could supply the words, and Van Meter gave him what he thought might be suitable.

Later in his room, Doane reviewed the poem and found it dreadful; he looked in his briefcase for something better. Then he knelt in prayer asking God to send him a poem for the event. In addition, he prayed something he had prayed several times before: he asked God to send him a poet who could write religious verse suitable for music.

While still on his knees, someone knocked on the door. As he opened it, a young boy handed him an envelope addressed to him. Tearing the envelope open, Doane read the letter: "Mr. Doane: I have never met you, but I feel impelled to send you this hymn. May God bless it." It was signed "Fanny Crosby." The following poem was enclosed:

> More like Jesus would I be,
> Let my Savior dwell with me,
> Fill my soul with peace and love,
> Make me gentle as the dove;
> More like Jesus as I go,
> Pilgrim, in this world below;
> Poor in spirit would I be—
> Let my Savior dwell in me.

The words seemed to lift off the page in song. Doane was thrilled. This would be the best poem for the mission anniversary—a song that asked God for grace to be more like Jesus. Doane immediately thought of a melody to go with the poem, and once more he prayed, thanking God for His answer.

The following day at the mission, Van Meter pumped the organ as Doane played and sang the hymn. The song so affected Van Meter that he burst into tears, came from behind the organ, and threw his arms around Doane's neck, crying, "Oh, Doane, where did you get that poem?"

When Doane told him the author's name, Van Meter gave him her address. Unable to meet with Fanny at that time, he resolved to do it the next time he was in the city.

Meanwhile, Bradbury was dying of consumption, so he had urged Fanny to send Doane her latest poem. Bradbury also asked Fanny, as he said good-bye to her, to "take up my life's work where I lay it down." He had hoped she would become the leader of the Sunday school hymn movement after his death.

Bradbury died in January 1868 at the age of fifty-one. At his funeral, as Bradbury had requested, the choir sang the first hymn he and Fanny had written together: "We Are Going, We Are Going to a Home Beyond the Skies." Walking by the casket, a distraught Fanny broke down in tears. Then she heard a mysterious voice "clear and beautiful," say to her, " 'Fanny, pick up the work where Bradbury has left it. Take your harp from the willow and dry your tears.' " Others standing by heard the voice but had no idea as to its source.

9

The Common Touch

William B. Bradbury and Company went through a reorganization after Bradbury's death; Sylvester Main and a local merchant, Lucius Horatio Biglow, became the new partners. The two men were primarily businessmen, so they left writing poetry and music to their employees. Fanny soon became their most outstanding writer. She had just the right flair for the new style of hymn that was becoming popular. Though she did not write the music for her words, she was allowed some say as to its suitability.

William Howard Doane returned to New York a short time after Bradbury's funeral and went to see Fanny. He could not believe the squalor she lived in, but she assured him that she wanted to live with the poor so she could minister to them. They had a pleasant talk, and as Doane left he pressed a bill into her hand. She thought it was $2, but later discovered it to be $20. Doane's visit was significant, and he and Fanny not only became colleagues but also close personal friends. Doane would provide the music for over a thousand of Fanny's hymns.

Although Doane was not an outstanding musician, Fanny liked to work with him. His tunes were usually simple, straightforward, marchlike tunes, and his catchy melodies were patterned after songs like "Hail to the Chief" and "Columbia, the Gem of the Ocean." People in the mid-1800s had to memorize a tune when they first heard it, since the chances of their hearing it again were rare. Without recordings and with few pianos, songs could only be heard in a few places, the church being one of them.

Some days after their first meeting, Doane came to see Fanny again and asked her if she could write a poem using the phrase "Pass me not, O gentle Savior." She promised him she would but was uninspired for several weeks. Then in the spring of 1868 she spoke at religious services in a prison. During one of the services, an inmate cried out in fear, "Good Lord! Do not pass me by!"

That night Fanny was able to write these words:

Pass me not, O gentle Savior,
Hear my humble cry,
While on others Thou art smiling,
Do not pass me by.
Savior, Savior,
Hear my humble cry,
While on others Thou art calling,
Do not pass me by.

Fanny sent Doane the words, and he soon composed a tune. A few days later the hymn was sung at the prison where Fanny continued to hold services. The song greatly impressed the prisoners, some being converted then and there. Touched by the men's reaction, Fanny fainted and had to be carried out.

Doane appeared at Fanny's home once more on April 30, announcing, "I have exactly forty minutes before I must meet a train for Cincinnati. I have a tune for you. See if it says anything to you. Perhaps you can commit it to memory and then compose a poem to match it." With that, he hummed a simple, touching melody.

As she listened, Fanny began to clap her hands, as she did when something pleased her. "Why, that says, 'Safe in the arms of Jesus!'" Usually Fanny's best hymns came when the tunes "spoke" to her.

Hurrying to another room in her little apartment, Fanny knelt on the floor, as was her custom before composing, and asked God for inspiration. The Lord sent the answer quickly. Fanny had the complete poem within half an hour. She maintained that during the time she was "wholly unconscious" of her surroundings and of everything except the hymn, which took shape in her mind without her own effort. Fanny said again later that she had nothing to do with writing the hymn; it was entirely the work of the "Blessed Holy Spirit."

Coming back to Doane in the other room, she repeated,

> Safe in the arms of Jesus,
> Safe on His gentle breast,
> There, by His love o'ershaded,
> Sweetly my soul shall rest.
> Hark! 'tis the voice of angels,
> Borne in a song to me,
> Over the fields of glory,
> Over the jasper sea.
> Safe in the arms of Jesus,
> Safe on His gentle breast,
> There, by His love o'ershaded,
> Sweetly my soul shall rest.

The hymn became an immediate hit. Biglow and Main included it in a hymnal three years later, and it was sung all over the country.

Fanny claimed a special fondness for "Safe in the Arms of Jesus." It had been written, she said, for "dead relatives" and for mothers who had lost their children. Possibly she had the memory of her own deceased child in mind when she wrote it.

The next year Doane asked Fanny to his home for the first of many visits. While in Cincinnati, she spoke to a group of workingmen. As she neared the end of her talk, she had an overwhelming sensation that "some mother's boy" listening to her "must be rescued that night or not at all." Thus she pleaded, "If there is a dear boy here tonight who has perchance wandered away from his mother's home and his mother's teaching, would you please come to me at the close of the service?"

At the meeting's close, a young man of about eighteen approached her asking, "Did you mean me?" He told Fanny he had made a promise to his mother to meet her in heaven, "but the way I have been living, I don't think that will be possible now."

Fanny prayed fervently for the young man, and "he finally arose with a new light in his eyes and exclaimed, 'Now I can meet my mother in heaven, for now I have found her God!'"

Later that evening Fanny thought of the hymn Doane had asked her to write on the home missions' theme "Rescue the Perishing." Before she went to bed, she had composed the complete hymn. The first stanza reads:

Rescue the perishing,
Care for the dying,
Snatch them in pity from sin and the grave;
Weep o'er the erring one,
Lift up the fallen,
Tell them of Jesus, the mighty to save.

When Fanny presented the poem to Doane the following day, he quickly gave it a rousing melody. It was published the next year in his *Songs of Devotion* and became a battle cry for home missions' workers everywhere.

Two of the nation's largest hymn publishers were Biglow and Main of New York and the John Church

Company of Cincinnati. Starting in the late 1860s, Fanny provided between a third and a half of the hymns for the New York company. In fact, the company urged her to use pen names so the public wouldn't realize that only one poet had written so many of their hymns.

Fanny liked being in great demand as a hymn writer, and she had no trouble producing enough hymns to meet her quotas. In forty-seven years she would provide Biglow and Main with 5,959 hymns (about two thousand of which were published). When a certain topic was proposed to her, Fanny would compose two or three poems and give the musicians their choice.

Fanny wrote for other publishers as well. She supplied several poems for Philip Phillips's *Musical Leaves* (1868), and she wrote at least twenty hymns for Phoebe Knapp for the book *Notes of Joy*. Fanny's popularity by the early 1870s would soon pave the way for the title "Queen of Hymn Writers."

In 1873 one of Fanny's employers, Sylvester Main, died at the age of fifty-six. But within three years she would meet Dwight L. Moody, the renowned American evangelist, and through Moody's soloist, Ira Sankey, her reputation would become even more prestigious. Indeed, before they met, Sankey made prolific use of her hymns in evangelistic campaigns.

When Moody began a series of evangelistic meetings in the British Isles, thousands professed faith in Christ. Even British royalty such as Alexandra, the Princess of Wales, confessed to being "greatly helped" by Moody's preaching. Moreover, through Sankey's poignant singing, the British public became enamored with Sunday school hymns. Sankey used many of Fanny's hymns like "Pass Me Not, O Gentle Savior," which gained tremendous popularity. And overnight Fanny's name became a household word in Great Britain.

Meanwhile, Fanny was in the midst of a speaking

tour that took her to Cincinnati, where she visited in the Doane home. At twilight one evening, she and Doane were talking about the nearness of God. The setting sun and gathering shadows affected both of them as they thought about God's goodness. Fanny was able to see enough light to appreciate the beauty all around her, which she sensed showed the glorious hand of God. As she retired, she was almost ecstatic over the scene she had just witnessed and wrote the words to "I Am Thine, O Lord." Published the following year, it quickly became a favorite.

In 1875 Fanny was fifty-five years old. She and her husband had moved to the East Side, which was closer to her office at Biglow and Main. That year marked the beginning of an important event in New York: Moody and Sankey organized an evangelistic campaign in Brooklyn.

10

Undisputed Title

In 1874 Fanny had been introduced to Philip P. Bliss, an outstanding hymn composer. The religious world had been quite taken with Bliss and his many captivating tunes such as "Hold the Fort." Bliss differed from Fanny in that he wrote his own music as well as verse. His hymnbooks, which he edited himself, were published by the John Church Company. Very seldom did Bliss compose tunes for other people's poems.

With Bliss's exceptional bass voice and musical talent, it wasn't long before he came to the attention of D. L. Moody, who urged him to become a full-time evangelist. The decision was a difficult one for Bliss, as he had begun to receive sufficient royalties from his hymns to provide a comfortable living. If he went into evangelism, there would be little time left for himself. But he finally acquiesced to Moody's wish, accepting it as God's will.

The same year, Sankey and Bliss collaborated on their hymns to produce *Gospel Hymns and Sacred Songs*, a hymnbook published jointly by the John Church Company and Biglow and Main. Fanny valued Bliss's musical abilities and hoped for the opportunity to work with him on some hymns, but at the time, Bliss indicated he had no need of new poetry to set to music. He then turned his attention to D. L. Moody's meetings in New York City, and Fanny decided to wait for another opportunity to work with the musician.

On October 24, 1875, opening day for D. L. Moody's New York campaign, the streets were filled with people by seven o'clock in the morning outside the Brooklyn Rink. Later that evening, Moody whipped his listeners into a frenzy as he preached on "Let us go up at once and possess it, for we are well able to overcome it." His talk of a revival in New York City brought loud exclamations of "Yes!" and "Amen!" from the listeners. Moody harped on the unbelief of established churches that, according to him, thwarted God's work. Those who doubted the possibility of a New York revival could be compared to the Israelites who were afraid to "go up and take the land." Moody emphasized, "When we *believe*, we are able to overcome giants and walls and everything!" The audience cheered and applauded his words.

As Moody closed, Sankey sang Bliss's "Only an Armor-Bearer." Then following the benediction, bands of young people rushed from the building and marched down Fulton Street, their arms interlocked as they sang Bliss's "Hold the Fort . . . for I am coming."

Fanny undoubtedly attended some of Moody's meetings that year, but she officially met Moody and Sankey the following year, in 1876, when they were in New York. They had used Fanny's hymns everywhere they went, and it was through the Moody campaigns that her name became known to mass audiences.

Moody was not at all musical either in playing an instrument or in singing. In fact, his singing was dreadful! But he loved to hear good music and was keenly aware of its importance in evangelization. Like Fanny, Moody believed the Gospel could be sung into people's consciousness—especially those not easily reached by the preached word. As a result, he insisted on giving as much time to the song service as to the preaching.

Moody and Sankey, realizing the power of Fanny's hymns, were eager for her to supply as many as they needed for their services. They recognized her as one of the greatest contemporary hymn writers, and Sankey began to fill new editions of *Gospel Hymns and Sacred Songs* with Fanny's verse. Moreover, by joining with Biglow and Main, Sankey was able to secure the rights to many of Fanny's earlier hymns. He also scheduled her to write new ones, and he began to compose melodies for many of her poems.

Fanny's hopes of collaborating with Philip Bliss ended abruptly at Christmas 1876, when he was killed instantly in a train wreck. Bliss's death at age thirty-eight "cast a cloud" over Fanny's spirit. Nevertheless, Fanny and her colleagues at Biglow and Main spent their time editing Bliss's last hymns, a joint venture between Biglow and Main and the John Church Company in Cincinnati.

Of course, Fanny had long ago learned to accept whatever came her way. She trusted God to work everything out for good. She continued to write various lyrics to celebrate birthdays, anniversaries, and other occasions; she also composed secular songs, and even love lyrics.

But Fanny was a woman of many interests, and something she enjoyed doing almost as much as writing poetry was speaking to people. For some of her engagements, she had to travel away from New York, but that never bothered her. She traveled alone and felt perfectly safe. Fanny's talks were like her hymns: simple, direct, and personal. The quality of intimacy, along with the love and joy she radiated in mid-life, touched people and made her a sought-after speaker. No one seemed to mind waiting for hours to hear her simple message.

Fanny would stand at the podium and give her famous greeting: "God bless your dear hearts! I'm so happy to be with you!" In her hands she held a small book, which many thought contained Braille; she would confide, however, that the book only served as a form of security. A typical talk was something like this one:

> My friends, I am shut out of the world, and shut in with my Lord! I have served Him as I could. As I have listened to the remarks made tonight [by the one who introduced her], I have thought, *Not unto me, O Lord, but unto Thee, be all the glory!* The Lord is the sunshine of my soul. I do not want to live for myself, but for Him. I remember my grandmother, as I knelt by her chair in which she rocked me to sleep and taught me to pray that if it was His will, to give me what I wanted, but if the Lord did not want me to have a thing, it was best not to have it. My friends, it is so good to be loved! Loved by God's own people! The memory of this meeting will never fade from my mind! When I go home and look into my Father's face and see the sunshine of His smile, my feelings will be like the tender affection and gratitude that glows in my heart now for you.

Although her talks tended to be brief and rambling, they were also heartfelt and inspiring. In addition, Fanny would recite one of her poems—sometimes composing one on the spot. Then she would close with the Mizpah benediction: "May the Lord watch between me and thee, when we are absent, one from the other."

Warmth and holiness radiated from Fanny to the point that it did not matter much what she said. People just liked to be near her and be uplifted and encouraged by her presence. She could cheer the despondent, awaken the lukewarm to a deeper commitment, and challenge the agnostic to come to Christ. Fanny's audiences were smaller than some of the other popular preachers, largely because she shunned publicity, but

she was ranked as one of the most effective evangelists
of her day.

Fanny's perpetual energy stood her well, and she
seemed never to tire. She was small and somewhat delicate but never suffered from a serious illness. In her old
age, she was known to wear out people twenty and
thirty years younger. Despite her energy, though, even
Fanny needed a vacation occasionally.

In the summer of 1877, some friends treated her to
a trip to Ocean Grove, New Jersey. The Methodists held
a camp meeting there, and people came from New York,
Philadelphia, and Trenton, New Jersey, to listen to messages, but also to enjoy fishing, swimming, and just
strolling along the beach. Fanny took the two-hour train
ride by herself, and some kind fellow passengers she
met on the train escorted her to her friends' place near
the beach.

Evening surfing provided the camp meeting highlight, which took place at sunset at the water's edge. Although Fanny could barely make out the faint rays of
the setting sun, she was as moved by the grandeur as
anyone. At the service, she enjoyed meeting John Rob-
son Sweney. People knew him as both a band leader and
a hymn writer.

Sweney benefited from a fine musical background
and led the singing at numerous evangelical camp meetings. He liked light, bouncy, lively tunes and had already composed a number of popular hymns and published several hymnals. Sweney was delighted to meet
Fanny at the camp meeting and asked her to supply
words for more of his tunes, which she agreed to do. The
rest and relaxation at Ocean Grove did Fanny a world
of good, and she returned to New York refreshed and
rested, ready to continue with her grueling schedule.

Fanny was now in great demand as a hymn writer.
She teamed up with several other popular writers of the

day such as William James Kirkpatrick, known as "Kir-
kie," who was a friend of Sweney, and a little later she
became acquainted with George Coles Stebbins, another composer. Fanny supplied Sweney and Kirkpatrick with over a thousand hymns; at the same time,
she provided Sankey with poems for his *Gospel Hymns*
hymnbook. Stebbins, a largely self-taught musician, set
many of Fanny's poems to music as they worked together over the following decades, but his style did not
always do Fanny's hymns justice. On the other hand,
some of the appealing hymn tunes he and Fanny collaborated on were very successful, such as "Jesus Is Calling" and "Saved by Grace."

Fanny had written the majority of her more famous
hymns by this time. In a span of nine years, she had
written "Safe in the Arms of Jesus," "Blessed Assurance," "Pass Me Not, O Gentle Savior," "Jesus, Keep Me
Near the Cross," "I Am Thine, O Lord," "All the Way My
Savior Leads Me," "Close to Thee," "Praise Him! Praise
Him!" "To God Be the Glory," "Every Day and Hour," and
"Rescue the Perishing." With two or three exceptions,
the hymns she wrote in her remaining years never approached her output during this fruitful period.

One may ask why this was true. Was Fanny Crosby
burned out? Perhaps. Whatever poems and hymns she
wrote following her years of extreme productivity
tended to paraphrase what she had already written. But
even these enjoyed moderate success and were generally better than those of her contemporaries. Moreover,
Fanny continued to be in demand as a lyricist, and her
main goal in life was to do the Lord's work. She knew
that He had called her to keep on doing the same tasks.
If her hymns helped one person or led one person to
Christ, that was enough for her.

She experienced another tragic loss in the spring of
1879 when her English friend and fellow hymn writer,

Frances Ridley Havergal, died in Wales at the age of forty-two. Fanny was sixty; she had outlived Philip Bliss and Frances Havergal, making her the unrivaled "Queen of Gospel Hymn Writers." But Fanny cared little what people thought of her; she was more interested in pleasing the Lord. Besides her hymn writing, she had at this time become a dedicated home mission worker, and each week she spent several days working in New York's Bowery district.

11

Missions Work

The wretched conditions of New York's tenements had drawn Fanny's attention for some time. She gave vent to her desire to be more involved with the people who lived there.

By the early 1880s Fanny resided in a dingy apartment on Frankfort Street on the Lower East Side, near one of Manhattan's worst slum areas. A few blocks away was an area known as the Bowery. The street by the same name was once the road to Peter Stuyvesant's *bouwerij*, or farm. In the mid- to late 1800s, however, this section of town had become home to alcoholics, prostitutes, and derelicts of all kinds. Taverns, dance halls, and sordid shops peddling obscene pictures could be found at every turn. So-called concert halls lured the curious to burlesque shows, and salesmen pitched "dime museums" to passersby. At one shop people paid to watch a man called Jack the Rat bite the heads off living rats. Civil War veterans without arms or legs or eyes crowded the streets, begging for scraps of bread.

A home mission effort at that time was usually manned by a team of Christian workers who ministered to the downtrodden around them. But one of the most dynamic missions in the area was the Water Street Mission, located near the East River and the yet-to-be-completed Brooklyn Bridge. Jerry McAuley, a young converted alcoholic, started the mission. McAuley was from a broken home and was nearly illiterate. His family had sent him to live with relatives in New York at the age of fourteen, and he soon became involved with a street gang. At nineteen he was falsely accused of highway robbery, serving five years at Sing Sing Penitentiary before his innocence was discovered and his freedom restored.

In time McAuley became a fervent Christian and wanted to help people in situations similar to his, so he founded the Water Street Mission. Ten years later he founded Cremorne-McAuley Mission on West 32nd Street. The three-story building housed a chapel, a kitchen, and living quarters where homeless and unemployed men were fed, clothed, and given the Gospel. While McAuley made certain the men heard the Good News, he never insisted on their conversion to Christ, as was the policy of some missions. These refused to feed or clothe people until they professed Christ. Because of his exemplary methods in helping men, McAuley enjoyed a favorable reputation. When a man left Sing Sing, for example, prison authorities would counsel him, "You had better go down and see McAuley at the Water Street Mission."

McAuley's missions became favorite places for Fanny to minister. She thought McAuley did an outstanding job. She remarked that "as a speaker, he uses simple language, but his manner is so impressive that all men are drawn to him."

Other missions blessed by Fanny's ministry and counsel were the Bowery Mission, founded in 1879 by Reverend Albert Rulifson, and the Door of Hope Mission, a mission started for "fallen women" by Mrs. E. M. Whittemore. Sometimes Fanny would be asked to speak when she visited these places. She was always happy to share the joy of "walking in the light." After speaking, she would urge the people to come forward and give their lives to Christ, then mingle with the audience and counsel as she could.

After speaking at the Bowery Mission one evening, Fanny closed with "If there is a man present who has gone as far as he can go, he is the person with whom I want to shake hands."

While Fanny waited, a man started slowly forward. When he got to the front, she asked him if he wanted "to come out and live a Christian life."

"Aw, what's the difference?" he responded. "I ain't got no friends. Nobody cares for me."

"You're mistaken," Fanny returned, "for the Lord Jesus cares for you—and others care, too! Unless I had a deep interest in your soul's welfare, I certainly would not be here talking with you on this subject."

Then she pointed him to several Scripture passages. Showing an interest in what she said, the man said he would come the next evening and sign the pledge not to use alcohol. Then he asked her, "Will you come with me?"

"Yes," she told him. "I will be here again tomorrow. And although I don't want to discourage you from signing the pledge, it seems to me that the best pledge you can make is to yield yourself to God."

Returning the next evening, the man responded to the message, and Fanny noted that "before the close of the meeting, we saw new light in his eyes and a change in his voice."

At this time in her life, Fanny considered mission work her principal occupation. The hymns she wrote simply extended her mission activities. Many of them were written especially to be used in the missions, as they urged a person to make a decision for Christ, and offered hope to the downcast.

Fanny considered her work a labor of love, and she freely gave love to the people to whom she ministered. She would caution, "Don't tell me a man is a sinner. You can't save a man by telling him of his sins. He knows them already. Tell him there is pardon and love waiting for him. Win his confidence and make him understand that you believe in him, and never give him up!"

If love was the main ingredient of Fanny's ministry, kindness rated a close second. She maintained that kindness helps others not only to come to faith "but to grow in grace day by day. There are many timid souls whom we jostle morning and evening as we pass them by. But if only a kind word were spoken, they might become fully persuaded."

Fanny tried to be careful not to offend anyone in her mission work, and she called all the men with whom she worked "my boys." She worked with numerous trainmen through the YMCA for many years, and she would gushingly say about them, "They are all my boys, and I love them all!" Even the evil smell of the men at the Bowery and Water Street Missions did not bother Fanny. She overlooked the nauseating odors of alcohol and tobacco, instead focusing on the human being and his needs. Of these men, she remarked, "Not one of them was ever ugly to me."

Fanny's favorite mission was the Bowery Mission, and much of her time was spent there. For sixteen straight years she gave their anniversary address. The men who had been converted and rehabilitated by the mission's ministry would return as guests of honor.

A special ministry opened up for Fanny in 1880 when her friend William Rock invited her to his home. Rock presided over the New York Surface Car Line and expressed concern about his employees. The men worked long hours, seven days a week, he told Fanny.

Few people spoke kindly to them, and they endured abuse from ill-tempered riders. These men, because of the long work hours and low pay, were often unhappy and difficult to be around. But Rock, concerned about their spiritual condition, got in touch with Fanny.

The two agreed to prepare a waiting room for an hour-long service each Sunday morning for conductors and drivers. Fanny was delighted when asked to hold the services. Fanny spoke of the place as a "dingy little room made cheerful with a bit of red carpet and a few flowers and plants." She called them her "railroad boys" and reached out to them with all the love and consolation she could muster.

As word spread about her work with the streetcar conductors and bus drivers, a delegation from the newly formed Railroad Branch of the YMCA located in Hoboken, New Jersey, went to see her. The delegation wanted her to become a regular lecturer for their organization. From then on, Fanny went on speaking tours at YMCAs along the East Coast. Wherever she went and whatever she did, all her activities were linked with the hymns that flowed from within her spirit. And the special times she spent alone with her Lord fed the springs of her life.

12

Quiet Hours

F anny wrote many of her hymns during the hours around midnight. Only then did the building quiet down: the shuffle of feet on rickety stairs ceased, and the discordant voices piercing the tenement's paper-thin walls grew still. She found silence essential as she sought to hear God's voice speaking to her in her writing. Since she worked at Biglow and Main during the day, and increasingly had speaking engagements at night, the only time left was in the wee hours of the morning. Fortunately Fanny did not require much sleep, so she could use this time to draw near to the Lord.

She called these times when she experienced deep communion with the Lord "The Valley of Silence." The physical world seemed far away and the spiritual world intensely real.

Keenly aware of the need for these long times of quietness, Fanny explained their value to her:

> Most of my poems have been written during the long night watches, when the distractions of the day could not interfere with the rapid flow of thought. It has been my custom to hold a little book in my hand, and somehow or other the words seem to come more

promptly when I am so engaged. I can also remember more accurately when the little volume is in my grasp. . . . Sometimes a hymn comes to me by stanzas and needs only to be written down, but I never have any portion of a poem committed to paper until the entire poem is composed; then there is often much pruning and revising necessary before it is really finished.

Fanny admitted that during these times of quietness her soul was sometimes filled with inspiration so powerful she could not "find words beautiful enough or thoughts deep enough for expression."

Often she received the inspiration for hymns from these quiet hours, but others came to her from some singular inspiration concerning events in the material world. She would dwell on a given subject as she went about her daily work, sometimes for days, weeks, or months, until something occurred to prompt her writing about it. A friend's death, for instance, might lead to a hymn such as "The Morning Land." An occurrence at one of the missions might pique her interest in the subject of "The Blessed Feast."

Fanny attempted to unravel the mystery of hymn writing in the following explanation:

The most enduring hymns are born in the silences of the soul, and nothing must be allowed to intrude while they are being framed into language. Some of the sweetest melodies of the heart never see the light of the printed page. Sometimes the song without words has a deeper meaning than the more elaborate combinations of words and music. But in the majority of instances these two must be joined in marriage.

Moreover, the words and music need to complement each other or the resulting hymn will not be pleasing. Fanny makes clear, too, that "The mere fitting of words to a melody is by no means all that is necessary; it must be so well done as to have the effect of having been written especially for that melody."

For this to be true, the poet must put his thoughts, aspirations, and emotions into metrical form in a way that the music composer can readily grasp the spirit of the poem. Then he can write music that will perfectly express the poet's meaning. She stressed, too, that a "similar harmony of thought must exist between the composer of the melody and the poet when the music is written first."

Fanny offered the following example of an event providing material for a hymn. At the first of a month in 1874, Fanny's rent was due, and she had no idea how she would pay it. She decided then and there to pray about it and commit the matter to the Lord. Almost at once a man whom she had never met appeared, and after placing a $10 bill in her hand, he left. Of course, the ten dollars was the exact amount she needed to take care of the rent. Her gratitude to the Lord translated almost immediately into words for a hymn: "All the Way My Savior Leads Me." Later that evening Fanny composed the following verse:

All the way my Savior leads me;
What have I to ask beside?
Can I doubt His tender mercy
Who through life has been my guide?

Her musician friend Robert Lowry had given the initial topic to her, but the incident now inspired the poem.

Ira Sankey shared the story of a miner who had come forward in one of the campaigns in England and begged to be prayed for by the leader of the prayer service (which generally followed the evening service). The leader suggested he come back the next night since it was late, but the man refused to budge, nearly sobbing, "No! It must be settled tonight! Tomorrow may be too late!" To placate the miner, the leader prayed for him, and the man left the meeting "saved." The next day the man was killed in an explosion. The incident so moved Fanny that she wrote a hymn called "Shall I Be Saved Tonight?"

Sometime later Fanny was staying at the home of William and Sara Kirkpatrick in Germantown, Pennsylvania, along with several other guests. The group started a discussion on the transitory nature of their earthly lives. Fanny spoke up, "How soon we grow weary of earthly pleasures, however bright they may be."

With that, Kirkpatrick declared, "Well, we are never weary of the grand old song!"

Fanny grasped at once the rhythm of the words as being just right for a hymn. She asked the group, "But what comes next?" They looked at her in confused silence. Kirkpatrick looked somewhat bewildered.

"Why," she practically shouted, "glory to God, hallelujah!" Fanny then insisted Kirkpatrick sit at the piano and compose a melody for the words that came to her then and there:

> We are never, never weary of the grand old song,
> Glory to God, hallelujah!
> We can sing it in the Spirit as we march along,
> Glory to God, hallelujah!

After her mother died some years later, Fanny had a vision of her in heaven and felt compelled to write this verse:

> Over the river they call me,
> Friends that are dear to my heart,
> Soon I shall meet them in glory,
> Never, no never to part.

After a bout with depression in 1874, Fanny called out in exasperation, "Dear Lord, hold my hand!" She noted that almost immediately "the sweet peace that comes of perfect assurance returned to my heart, and my gratitude for the evidence of answered prayer sang itself into the lines of a hymn":

> Hold Thou my hand, so weak am I and helpless
> I dare not take one step without Thy aid;
> Hold Thou my hand, for then, oh, loving Savior,
> No dread of ill shall make my soul afraid.

On other occasions, a musician would play a melody and request that Fanny write words for it. She would listen closely to see if "the tune said something." If it did, she could write the appropriate words. If not, she would simply tell the composer that she couldn't write for a tune that "said nothing to her."

Many times it was difficult for Fanny to write when nothing inspired her. Biglow and Main set a quota of hymns for her, and to keep her job she had to comply. But later she would admit that "there were some days when I could not compose a hymn if all the world had been laid at my feet as recompense."

Doane, for instance, might request a New Year's hymn on December 30. A few months later, Hugh Main would ask, "I'd like you to compose twenty selections for my Easter collections and I'd like them in two weeks." Then Jerry McAuley needed "three invitational hymns" for his services at the mission.

Fanny rarely refused requests for hymns and did her best to write satisfactory ones. Her solution to being uninspired was to "build a mood—or try to draw one around me." Also to "pray to God to give me the thoughts and feelings wherewith to write my hymn." Then thankfully, "after a time—perhaps not unmingled with struggle—the ideas would come." She always wanted to be "in condition to reach the minds and hearts of my constituency and write something worthy of them." Sometimes she composed hymns and verses according to an earlier model such as "Sweet Hour of Prayer" or "Stand Up, Stand Up for Jesus."

Moreover, Fanny had to keep the hymn's "singability" in mind. Thus forming the right meter was very important to her: "For if there is a false accent or a mistake in meter, the hymn cannot stand much chance of proving a success, or at least its possibilities are very much lessened. Among the millions of hymns that have been sung and forgotten, many, no doubt, contained deep and pious thought and feeling, but have been crippled or killed by the roughness of some line or the irregularity of one or more measures."

If a tune did not exist initially, or if Fanny could not think of another on which to hang her verses, she tried meticulously to shape the verses "in such a manner that the composer of the music might readily grasp the spirit of the poem and compose notes that will perfect the expression of the poet's meaning." At times this situation became a problem since many of the men composing melodies for her verses were amateurs. But if a tune was provided for Fanny, she was usually able to rise to the occasion with her expertise as a writer of verse.

Fanny preferred, of course, to be given a tune instead of a topic. She could always write a good poem for a good tune, but if the tune was poor, she had the prerogative of rejecting it. On the other hand, when she wrote a good poem for a given topic, she could not guarantee it would be accompanied by a suitable tune.

When Fanny received divine inspiration for a poem, it usually came as a whole and quite rapidly. Without inspiration, of course, the process would be slower. Often her hymns came in stanzas, or verse by verse. In the case of "The Bright Forever," she struggled for two days without discovering a single line. All of a sudden, "almost in a twinkling, the words came, stanza by stanza, as fast as I could memorize them."

She usually finished the entire first draft in a single night—perhaps after two or three hours. If she had time, she liked to "let it lie for a few days in the writing desk of my mind, so to speak, until I have the leisure to prune it, to read through it with the eyes of my memory, and in other ways mold it into as presentable a shape as possible."

Fanny did not always have the luxury of pruning and revising her material because of the constant pressure to provide multiple poems in a short time. She experienced added pressure due to her habit of composing two or three poems for each topic or tune. This habit meant that many of her eight-thousand-plus hymns were composed in haste, making for mediocrity—or as hymnologist John Julian suggested, "weak and poor." Fortunately there were numerous times when Fanny was genuinely inspired and could write more leisurely. Under these circumstances, the hymns were of superior quality.

During her more productive years when Fanny composed large quantities of poetry, she dictated them to a secretary. Her employer, Hugh Main, related Fanny's unorthodox work methods: "She has her hymns written down for her, and she will dictate to two persons at once, or two lines of one poem to one person and two lines of another hymn to another person and never forget a word herself."

Any comments to Fanny about her amazing memory fell on deaf ears. Even though she had the ability to remember endless numbers of hymns and dictate them one after the other without any difficulty, she did not consider her memory superior to anyone else's. When people praised her great "talent," Fanny would likely deliver a lecture telling them she merely used the gift God had given her and that He gives to everyone. She maintained that most sighted people waste their memory through laziness. They depend on "memorandum tablets and carefully kept journals and ledgers," which, to Fanny, were "destructive to the books of the mind."

Biglow and Main, like most publishing houses, paid Fanny only one or two dollars for each hymn. Even when a hymn was very successful, she received nothing more than the original fee. The publisher claimed the words as his exclusive property, so no one else could write music for them.

Most of the time the composer made little money from the hymns since the publishing company kept most of the profits. Some people believed the publishers took advantage of Fanny and thought she should insist on more money for her songs. But Fanny felt that by composing hymns she was doing a favor for her fellowmen; and more importantly, she was doing what God called her to do. The fact that people were finding the Lord through her hymns was satisfaction enough.

13

Winning Souls

I f a popular song poll of the "top ten" hymns had been taken in the last twenty years of the nineteenth century, several of Fanny's hymns would surely have made the list. "Safe in the Arms of Jesus" was one of her hymns that was known and loved in many places. Translated into more than two hundred languages, it was sung and enjoyed around the world. "Blessed Assurance" also became extremely popular. In fact, Sankey deemed it "one of the most popular and useful" of all the songs used in Moody's evangelistic meetings.

Of "Pass Me Not, O Gentle Savior," Sankey said, "No other hymn in our collection was more popular than this at our meetings in London in 1874. It was sung every day at Her Majesty's Theatre in Pall Mall." It continued to be the evangelists' most popular hymn even after their return to the United States; it was also translated into several languages. New York minister Dr. E. I. Dakin said the hymn brought more souls to Christ than any other.

Other hymns that received much acclaim were "Rescue the Perishing," "Jesus, Keep Me Near the Cross," "I Am Thine, O Lord," and "All the Way My Savior Leads Me." Not only were Fanny's hymns appreciated in religious gatherings, but in secular circles as well. Numerous conversion stories circulated about her hymns touching people and speaking to them about their need for a Savior.

Fanny waited in eager anticipation to hear the stories of how her hymns moved people; not out of pride, but because she loved to see God work through music: "God has given me a wonderful work to do. A work that has brought me untold blessing and great joy. When word is brought to me, as it is from time to time, of some wandering soul coming home through one of my hymns, my heart thrills with joy and I give thanks to God for giving me a share in the glorious work of saving human souls."

God also used her hymns to encourage and comfort those who already believed. Sankey mentioned to her on one occasion, "You have been the means of cheering tens of thousands trudging along the highways of life."

One day following the church service, a woman approached Fanny, saying, "Oh, thank God, I have found you. I have prayed that I might see you before I die. 'Safe in the arms of Jesus' was the last thing my mother said before she went home." Sankey gave a comparable report about the hymn's blessing in Scotland in 1885: the hymn had led to numerous conversions and helped many individuals who were beset by problems.

When a teenage boy with an incurable illness sang "Blessed Assurance" in his hospital room, he helped fourteen other patients to find Christ. As he prepared to die, he sang "Safe in the Arms of Jesus." Then, as his soul departed, he called out, "Ma, I hear the voice of angels! Ma, there are the fields of glory! Ma, there is the jasper sea!"

"Rescue the Perishing," although written specifically for mission outreach and to motivate Christians in soul-winning, also helped many individuals to find

Christ. A striking instance of how useful the hymn was in soul-winning can be seen in the case of an alcoholic man roaming through the Bowery. Passing the Water Street Mission, he heard people singing the hymn and was drawn by the triumphant, persuasive melody. Then he went inside to hear it better and soon "broke down in contrition."

In another episode, an Englishman told Sankey that "Rescue the Perishing" was responsible for his conversion. He admitted to being "very far from my Savior, and living without a hope in Jesus. Yet I was very fond of singing hymns, and one day I came across this beautiful piece." The particular verse that touched him was the following:

> Touched by a loving heart,
> Wakened by kindness,
> Chords that were broken
> Will vibrate once more.

Another arresting incident took place at the Bowery Mission one evening. A drunk man dressed in shabby clothes wandered in from the street during the singing of "Rescue the Perishing." The speaker mentioned his Civil War experiences and the company in which he served.

When the service concluded, the drunken man staggered to the front and sought out the speaker, saying, "Do you remember the name of the captain of your company?" The speaker nodded, giving the man's name. "You are right," the drunk agreed, "I am that man! I *was* your captain! Now look at me today and see what a wreck I am! I have lost everything that I had in the world through drink and I don't know where to go. Can you save your old captain?" The man was soon professing Christ as his Savior and became a committed mission worker. He delighted in giving lectures on his thrilling conversion and credited "Rescue the Perishing" for his changed life.

Sankey knew a well-known Englishman who "had been very much opposed to our meetings, and his opposition was not lessened when he saw his wife converted." Nevertheless, the man agreed to go to the last meeting with her. In his own words, he admitted that he felt "touched by the Spirit of God" when he heard "Pass Me Not, O Gentle Savior."

Even some of Fanny's lesser-known hymns spoke to people. Riding on a trolley in the early 1870s, Fanny received inspiration for a hymn and composed the first verse straightaway:

> Jesus, I love Thee, Thou art to me
> Dearer than ever mortal can be;
> Jesus, I love Thee, Savior Divine,
> Earth has no friendship constant as Thine;
> Thou wilt forgive me when I am wrong,
> Thou art my comfort, Thou art my song!
> Jesus, I love Thee, yes, Thou art mine.
> Living or dying, still I am Thine!

The hymn greatly touched William Howard Doane, who was riding with Fanny that day, and in the evening he wrote a tune for it. Published in 1873, the hymn enjoyed a modest popularity. Several years later a British minister used the hymn for his closing invitation, and a visitor came forward to accept Christ. The woman soon became one of the most dedicated members the congregation had ever known. She believed the words to Fanny's hymn had brought light and life to her soul and wanted others to know and to share her new joy. Her sincere, dynamic witness was instrumental in twenty-four persons finding Christ the following year, after which she passed away. She asked the pastor on her deathbed to thank Fanny Crosby for writing "Jesus, I Love Thee."

Fanny also wrote a hymn called "Only a Step to Jesus," which led to a southerner's conversion. A country squire who enjoyed hymn-singing came to town one evening and stopped by a local church. The congregation was singing "Only a Step to Jesus," and the hymn spoke to his heart. He could not get the song out of his mind and even dreamed about the words that night. The following day, as he thought about the meaning of the words, he was led to examine his life and soon professed Christ as his Savior. In turn, many in the church who knew the man to be somewhat of a skeptic, wept profusely at his remarkable conversion and changed life.

A Pittsburgh Anglican church became witness to a thrilling conversion story. A woman from the congregation went forward one morning to give testimony as to what the Lord had done in her life. Testimonies were not a part of the Anglican service, and the woman's remarks astonished priests and parishioners alike. She said she had been a prostitute and happened to hear the hymn "Saved by Grace" at an outdoor evangelistic meeting. Listening to the hymn reminded the woman of her childhood and of her mother's prayers for her. Whereupon she knelt at the curbside and asked God's forgiveness: "Then and there I received it, and I left the place with a peace which has never forsaken me." The minister stepped down from the high altar and with tear-filled eyes wished her Godspeed. The parishioners claimed the atmosphere was so charged that morning that it seemed "the Lord Jesus himself had been there."

Why did these simple hymns have the effect they did on people? Fanny was always quick to say it was because the Holy Spirit wrote the hymns through her. Before she began writing a hymn, she would always pray and ask God to use it to lead many souls to Him. Further she prayed that she might be the means of saving more than a million men through her hymns.

No one would argue that her hymns were first-rate literature, but their effect on people proved phenomenal—often awaking great emotion. Known for their straightforwardness, the words were so simple a child could understand them, yet they were not trite. Their vividness came through the use of familiar phrases. Terms such as "sylvan bowers" and "vernal flowers" may have made for bad poetry but quite successful hymnody. Hymns, according to Fanny, were not "pure" poetry but more utilitarian; their purpose was to aid in worship.

Thus Fanny filled her hymns with stock phrases and familiar expressions such as "Rock of Ages," "saved by grace," "golden shore," and "bleeding side." Most of her hymns contained scriptural references such as "living bread" (John 6:35), waters "gushing from the rock" (Num. 20:11), "my Father's house above" (John 14:2), "the angel reapers" gathering in the harvest (Matt. 13:39), and the "pearly gates" (Rev. 21:21).

Fanny considered a hymn "a song of the heart addressed to God," and her hymns spoke to the hearts of those who sang them. She was able to relate her hymns to the worshiper's own experience: "Now there is pardon for *you*," "Pass *me* not," and "*I* come to Thee." She worked at keeping her hymns in the first person so that the people could sing them as a personal prayer or testimony.

One of the singular aspects of Fanny's hymns is the familiarity with which she addressed the Savior. In fact, her fondness for using the "familiar epithets" so denounced by Lowell Mason is obvious. Even today there are those who dislike her over-familiar tone in addressing Deity. But Fanny felt the familiar phrases and expressions testified to her belief in a strong, intensely personal relationship with God. Another factor to note is that the age in which she lived was an emotionally charged one—affection was openly shown. When Sankey sang, tears rolled down his cheeks; men had no qualms about weeping in public.

Fanny's familiar names for the Savior were also the outgrowth of the emotionally affectionate language with which she addressed her family and friends. Of course, the Savior had a special place in her heart, so the terms of endearment came naturally.

Fanny also used the literary device of repetition in her hymns. She would repeat a key word, a phrase, or figure of speech all the way through a hymn. By way of illustration, "Safe in the Arms of Jesus" repeats the word "safe" five times in three stanzas and twice in the chorus. Although worshipers may be unaware of the repetition, the word "safe" works in their subconscious until they genuinely feel they *are* safe in the arms of Jesus.

Some critics maintain that Fanny's hymns were successful not because of their words but because of their tunes. But Fanny did not mind criticism. In fact, she paid little attention to it. She composed hymns for the people and for her Lord. And she knew exactly the kind of hymn that the common person would enjoy and could best understand.

14

Heart Issues

When the Brooklyn Bridge opened in 1883, commuters could easily travel from New York City to the more suburban area of Brooklyn. Numerous people bought or built homes across the East River; George Coles Stebbins, along with his family, was one of them. Ira Sankey, too, moved with his wife and sons from Chicago to Brooklyn. Fanny was overjoyed with the possibility of being able to spend more time with these friends. George Stebbins' gentle, quiet ways pleased Fanny, and she spent much time in the Stebbins home; she referred to him as one of her "most devoted and precious friends."

Frequently the Stebbinses and Fanny met at the Sankey home. Given Sankey's high-strung temperament, which was similar to Fanny's, the two seemed well-suited to each other. After D. L. Moody, Fanny may have been Sankey's closest friend. Because of the new proximity Fanny had to Sankey, the two began to write more hymns together in the spacious parlor of his home. After Fanny provided the verses, Sankey attached a simple melody to them.

At this time (1883) Fanny moved to First Avenue and 79th Street. Since she could no longer attend the John

Street Methodist Church because of the distance, she soon joined the Cornell Memorial Church on 76th Street. It was the first church she ever officially joined.

Whether Van moved with Fanny is uncertain, but he did not seem to be part of her life at this time. In 1882 the couple was still together, though their different interests and circles of friends continued to pull them in opposite directions. According to Fanny, they still loved each other, but their relationship had changed from being husband and wife to simply good friends.

On March 24, 1884, Fanny was honored with the first of her annual birthday parties at the offices of Biglow and Main. She had worked for them for twenty years, having written over three thousand hymns. The firm decided she deserved special recognition and honor. Following a full-course meal, the program consisted of poetry written in Fanny's honor by Hugh Main, Sankey, Kirkpatrick, Lowry, Doane, and others. Hugh Main's comic poem became a staple at subsequent birthday gatherings.

D. L. Moody held a Christian convention on evangelism in New York in October 1884. The meetings took place at Lafayette Avenue Presbyterian Church in Brooklyn, and Sankey was very much a part of the convention. Moody had expressed concern about the personal evangelism of church members. He believed that if a revival was to take place, laymen had to do their part. He suggested that individual churches hold revivals regularly.

Although Fanny still wrote hymns for Biglow and Main during this time, her most successful hymn-writing was for Kirkpatrick and Sweney. Some of the many hymns she contributed to *Songs of Redeeming Love* (1882) and *Glad Hallelujahs* (1887) were "Tell Me the Story of Jesus," "Redeemed, How I Love to Proclaim It," and "We Are Never Weary of the Grand Old Song." Her most successful and popular song at this time, however, was "He Hideth My Soul in the Cleft of the Rock"; Kirkpatrick provided the music for the hymn.

In the late summer of 1879, D. L. Moody started what would become the first of his annual Northfield (Massachusetts) Christian Workers' Conferences. Moody enjoyed spending his summers reading the Bible and relaxing in the countryside surrounding his Northfield home. Unable to relax for long, Moody soon invited his friends and neighbors into the dining room for Bible readings. As was usually the case where Moody was concerned, so many people came they could not get into the house; the porch overflowed, with people peering in through the windows!

Moody was so encouraged by the interest shown in the Bible, he decided to set aside a week for Christian workers to come to Northfield to pray and study the Scriptures and to be renewed in their Christian commitment. At least three hundred people attended the first Northfield retreat in September 1879. The people stayed in the Northfield Seminary dormitory and for ten days studied "the doctrine of the Holy Spirit" and prayed for numerous Christian institutions.

Fanny had wanted to attend the meetings for some time, but the way did not open until 1886 when she stayed with the Sankeys in their summer home. She greatly enjoyed the meetings, which were held in tents and in the seminary chapel. Moody had asked her to speak, but she refused. She had refused to speak at Ocean Grove, too. After all, these respites from the city were her vacations—times when she could get away from the constant demands of addresses and talks and people. Going back to the stuffy air of the city was somewhat of a shock for Fanny after breathing "the mountain air so sweet."

Before long she became involved in working on a sentimental operetta called *Zanie*, which would see production the next year. Hart Pease Danks (1834–1903), a well-known composer, had hired Fanny as librettist. Danks had written a hit song earlier, "Silver Threads Among the Gold." Many of Fanny's contemporaries did not approve of the theater; in fact, Moody and Sankey refused to go, but she was quick to remind them that if the content was wholesome and edifying, there was nothing wrong with a play or opera or popular music. After writing *Zanie*, Fanny collaborated with Doane in a completely secular Christmas cantata called *Santa Claus*. Fanny took comfort in the introduction, which explained that "this cantata has a religious sentiment pervading it, intending to illustrate the triumph of right over wrong."

Fanny's two sisters, Carrie and Jule, lived in nearby Bridgeport, Connecticut; Carrie took care of their mother, Mercy. Both sisters' husbands had died in the 1880s; Carrie's husband, Lee Rider, in December 1883 at the age of thirty-six; and Jule's husband, Byron, of a weakened heart in December 1887 at the age of fifty.

Shortly after Byron's death, Fanny's only surviving aunt, Polly Decker, died of a heart attack at seventy. Since she was only two years older than Fanny and they had been constant playmates growing up, Fanny felt her loss keenly. Only one person remained in Fanny's life from the early days in Gayville: her mother, who was eighty-eight.

Thankfully a welcome invitation by former president Grover Cleveland cheered Fanny in March 1889. Cleveland had bought a home on Madison Avenue in New York, and invited Fanny to come for a visit. They renewed an acquaintance of thirty-five years earlier when Cleveland worked for a short time at the New York Institution for the Blind. Following the visit, Cleveland suggested that he and Fanny keep in touch.

Fanny wrote another forty hymns for Lowry and Doane's *Bright Array*, but none achieved much success. By now it seemed whatever Fanny produced was less than original. The quality of her hymns was deteriorating, but Biglow and Main wanted her to write more and more, so she gamely persevered. The company even asked her to write paraphrases of popular hymns by other authors such as "Wonderful Words of Life" and "Showers of Blessing." But Fanny's versions were quickly put aside by the public. At this time she wrote such a great number of hymns in quick succession and without adequate time or thought that she did not even recognize some of her own hymns when they were sung.

She only wrote half a dozen or so good hymns in the next quarter-century, but her fame continued to spread based on her previous accomplishments and her reputation as a preacher and lecturer. From then on, Fanny would be better known as a preacher, but her place was secure in the hearts of people as "the hymn writer" and as "the queen of gospel song."

15

Memories at Seventy

When D. L. Moody came back to New York in 1890 for his first major evangelistic campaign in the city since 1876, Fanny celebrated her seventieth birthday. Many things had changed in the intervening years. No longer did Moody have to engage the largest meeting halls. His middle-aged and older listeners fit nicely into the local churches. He expressed disappointment when he realized that the majority of his audience was already "saved." He complained that his meetings were attended by "chronic attendees of religious meetings, who crowd everybody else out." He sensed that he was looking at the same faces he had looked at a decade earlier.

Neither did Sankey accompany Moody for this campaign. His golden voice had given out before he reached the age of fifty. George Stebbins now served as Moody's soloist.

Moody referred to his meetings as "Bible readings." More and more he spoke in these meetings of the declining interest of religion in America. The earlier awakenings, beginning in the 1850s and peaking in the 1870s, had run their courses, and Moody was deeply concerned about the state of Christianity in America.

He pondered ways to make religion more acceptable to young people. Speaking from the pulpit at Marble Collegiate Church in 1890, he suggested that ministers make their sermons shorter and that they put more energy into their services. He further advocated that ministers not take "Reverend" for a title; that it was a title reserved for Christ. Ministers should be called "Mister" as others were.

Fanny went to the meetings but, as usual, refused any offers to speak. She got caught at one meeting, however, when she could not find a seat. She started to leave during the singing of "Blessed Assurance," when Will Moody came along telling her he would find her a seat; and he did—on the platform! Fanny took the incident in good humor as D. L. Moody raised his arms to interrupt the singing with "Praise the Lord, here comes the authoress!"

In May of 1890 Fanny spoke to a Decoration Day crowd at Seaside Park. She recited a poem she had written for the local post of the Grand Army of the Republic. Her appearance was so successful, she was asked to come back annually to repeat her performance. Fanny's Decoration Day poem and address became a much-looked-forward-to event by those who attended. (Later on, at the age of ninety, she would still touch the hearts of aging veterans and their families, often to the point of tears.)

The day after her first Decoration Day address, Fanny went to Bridgeport to celebrate her mother's ninetieth birthday. It was the highlight of the year for her close family. But in the summer Mercy became very ill and was taken to a hospital; the doctors said her condition was hopeless, and on September 1, with Fanny, Carrie, and Jule beside her bed, Mercy "passed peacefully from this world to the brighter home above."

Fanny was saddened, however, when her sisters declared themselves the "only heirs and next of kin" for Mercy's little estate. Fanny, as always, shrugged her shoulders and went her way. She always knew God would provide for her needs, and that was enough.

As if to compensate for her grief, the Lord allowed Fanny to write two hymns the following year that were quite successful. Sweney had asked her to "write something tender and pathetic." He had a tune in mind that sounded very much like "She'll Be Comin' Round the Mountain," accompanied by a peppy brass band.

As Fanny prayed for illumination for the hymn, she received the words to "My Savior First of All." Before long nearly everyone in America and in England was singing the song.

The second popular song came to Fanny shortly after her cousin Howard Crosby, a well-known Presbyterian pastor, died in New York City. It happened that Lucius Biglow looked at a pamphlet containing the late pastor's last message. It stated that no Christian need fear death: "If each of us is faithful to the grace that is given to us by Christ, that same grace, which teaches us how to live, will also teach us how to die."

Fanny, in a burst of inspiration, quickly wrote a poem titled "Some Day." She passed it on to Biglow, who paid her two dollars and put the hymn in their vault. Fanny thought perhaps the poem would be forgotten like many of the others she had written. But with some minor changes, this poem that Fanny considered her "heart's song" would become the well-known "Saved by Grace."

Fanny soon became friends with the assistant pastor of Cornell Methodist Church. His name was Gerhard Johannes Schilling. Born in Germany, he experienced a dramatic conversion in Burma. Shortly after his conversion, he lost his job and moved to New York to attend divinity school. Every Sunday and Wednesday evening,

Schilling would pick up "Aunt Fanny" in his carriage for church. He also came to know and love her hymns.

In 1894 Fanny spent the summer in Northfield with the Sankeys. The Moodys were in Europe for the summer, and Dr. Adoniram Judson Gordon, a renowned Baptist minister and writer, was leading the annual conference. After one of Gordon's addresses on the Holy Spirit, Ira Sankey approached Fanny, asking, "Will you say something? There is a request from the audience that you speak."

Fanny shook her head, saying, "Oh, Sankey, I cannot speak before such an array of talent!"

Then Gordon spoke up, "Fanny, do you speak to please man or God?"

Her conscience touched, Fanny said, "Why, I hope to please God!"

"Well, then," responded Gordon, "go out and do your duty."

After taking her place at the podium, Fanny made a few remarks, then quoted her "heart's song," the poem "Some Day." She began:

> Some day my earthly house will fall,
> I cannot tell how soon 'twill be,
> But this I know, my All in All
> Has now a place in heaven for me.

As Fanny finished, a wave of both quiet emotion and sobbing swept over the auditorium.

Stebbins later asked Fanny to add a chorus:

> And I shall see Him face to face,
> And tell the story—saved by grace.

The poem was set to a slow tune, and though not particularly delicate or melodic, Fanny's "heart's song" became a favorite among evangelical Christians all over the world. Upon his return, Moody heard the hymn and loved it. It became a hit song of the Gay Nineties and seemed to be on everyone's lips.

Her "heart's song," however, was to be Fanny's last truly popular hymn.

16

Fanny's Story

During the 1890s, Fanny's friend and colleague Robert Lowry wanted to do something to provide an income for Fanny's final years since the demand for hymns and hymnals was declining. Fanny had never earned much money; her yearly income had averaged about $400, which was a small income even in those days. Doane and Lowry were collaborating on *The Royal Hymnal*, one that would be their last, and Lowry planned to have Fanny publish another poetry collection called *Bells at Evening*. The volume would contain selections from three earlier works, now out of print, plus a biographical sketch of Fanny by Lowry. The collection included several of Fanny's secular poems along with what she considered to be her best hymns. The finished book of 224 pages sold for fifty cents a copy, and Biglow and Main made certain the profits went to Fanny. Sales were fairly brisk, and there were several printings.

Nevertheless, some of Fanny's friends believed she had been taken advantage of by her employers. They felt she had never been adequately compensated for her many outstanding hymns. Other people assumed she should be well-off like some of her peers. Moody owned a fine home in Northfield, and Sankey had a home in Brooklyn, plus a summer home in Northfield.

Phoebe Knapp, probably Fanny's wealthiest friend, was determined to do something to secure Fanny's future. When she offered Fanny outright monetary gifts, Fanny always refused them. So Phoebe went to Will Carleton, a poet and author of several volumes of popular sentimental verse and editor of the magazine *Every Where*. Carleton had known and loved Fanny for a number of years and greatly admired her work. Phoebe suggested that he write down the story of Fanny's early life from her dictation and publish it in serial form in *Every Where*. Carleton agreed to it. Some of the articles' profits would go to Fanny, which would help her financially without her thinking she was accepting charity.

When Carleton visited Fanny's dingy apartment, he was shocked by the terrible conditions. Of course, Fanny didn't really suffer want, but Carleton thought her apartment inappropriate for her status and reputation.

Fanny dictated her story as planned, and Carleton wrote it down for the magazine. With her permission, the articles were published in *Every Where* over a period of months, and Fanny received $10 for each article.

But Fanny's employers—Hugh Main, William Howard Doane, and others at Biglow and Main—were irritated because Carleton and Phoebe Knapp insinuated they were not paying Fanny enough money. They were quick to point out that Fanny was receiving far more from *Bells at Evening* than from Carleton's articles. They also thought the articles actually hurt Fanny by competing with the poetry book.

In time the bickering between Biglow and Main and Carleton and Phoebe would boil over, causing damage to all parties concerned. What they failed to consider was that Fanny chose to live as she did. She appreciated her friends' help, but she had little use for wealth. At any time she could have insisted that Biglow and Main pay her more; other hymn writers got $10 for each hymn. But she always settled for a minimum payment and was happy with it. In addition, Fanny never set a standard fee for her services as a speaker, and she often refused the honorarium. When anyone insisted she take money, she would usually protest that they were paying her too much. Later she would give away what little she had and pray for her daily needs of food, rent, and other necessities.

Fanny's good friend D. L. Moody suggested to Main that instead of paying Fanny per hymn, he pay her a weekly salary of $8. Now Fanny's yearly income rose to $416—about what she had been making. Both Moody and Main realized that in the very near future Fanny would not be writing many hymns but her salary would continue.

Fanny's friends could not be blamed for their concern. Nearly eighty, Fanny did not look well. They were also worried about her living by herself. Her sisters wanted her to come live with them in Bridgeport, but Fanny was fiercely independent and refused.

She did suffer some mishaps during this time, which only served to nourish her friends' and family's anxiety for her. While visiting the Moodys in Northfield, Fanny fell down some steps and was badly cut. After recovering from the accident, she had a heart attack in Brooklyn, and for some time her life hung in the balance. She amazed everyone with a complete recovery but disdained the promptings of her family and doctors to rest.

Fanny quickly resumed her evening work in the New York missions. She also continued to travel and speak throughout New England, insisting she needed no one to accompany her. She had wished to revisit the scenes of her childhood for some time, so in the summer of 1897 she went to her old home in Gayville. Fanny received an invitation while there to speak to the graduating women of Drew Seminary, which was located in nearby Carmel. Fanny delighted her audience reminiscing about her youth in the area.

The month of August that year found Fanny in central New York. She had been named poet laureate of the Chautauqua Circle at Tully Lake, and as such she would attend their summer Round Table and give at least one poetic address. Assembly Park, near Syracuse, was where Fanny would speak. The guests considered her the star attraction.

Not only did Fanny charm the audiences at Tully Lake, but she also found time to speak at a number of surrounding places such as a rescue mission, the state fair, an Indian reservation, the Elmwood Grange—a home for the elderly, and a church. It seemed she was never still.

But Fanny did find time to relax at the conference. Her friend Eliza Hewitt went to the Round Table every year and proved to be a most desirable and delightful companion for Fanny; the two were nearly like sisters.

Fanny stayed with the John Roberts family at this conference. Her hosts realized she needed time to prepare her poems and speeches, so they tried to keep the continuous stream of callers away. Fanny, however, wanted to greet her "friends" and always took time to see them.

While the popularity of evangelists like D. L. Moody declined in the 1890s, Fanny's reputation appeared to grow. This may have been because she took time to speak to small groups of people, whereas Moody generally addressed larger groups in churches and auditoriums. Fanny may have also come across as a more caring personality than Moody and others like him. Preachers of the day concentrated on telling people of their sins, scolding and chiding them. Fanny, on the contrary, wanted to share the love of God with people and chose to give them hope and comfort instead of constantly warning them.

Other factors that drew people to Fanny were her blindness and the indefinable charisma and mystique that she possessed. People were fascinated by her, and even those who criticized her hymns had to admit that Fanny had a unique charm about her, even an aura of holiness.

17

Lasting Friendships

Many of Fanny's friends and composers who had helped her create her greatest hits had begun to pass from the scene. Some of them—Chester Allen, Silas Vail, and William Sherwin—had already died; then John Sweney had a stroke a short time after Moody's New York campaign and died in April 1899. Not long afterward Robert Lowry was confined to bed with a serious illness. When Fanny went to visit him, they talked about bygone years and events. Finally the dying man turned to her and spoke somberly, "Fanny, I am going to join those who have gone before. My work is done."

Fanny could not speak for her sadness. She recalled, "I simply took his hand in mine and said quietly, 'I thank you, Dr. Lowry, for all that you have done for me.' " Then she added these words that echoed an earlier hymn they had co-written: "Good-night, until we meet in the morning." Lowry passed away on November 25 of that year.

With many of the older generation of hymn writers gone, a new generation was coming to take their place. Some of them had a style very similar to that of their predecessors. Charles Hutchison Gabriel, from Iowa, could probably be called the successor to Lowry, Doane,

Sankey, Sweney, and Kirkpatrick. Although he was completely self-taught, Gabriel's hymns were simple and had what was known as "the old Methodist swing." He often wrote his own words, crediting the lyrics to pen names such as "Charlotte G. Homer" and others.

In time Gabriel asked Fanny to provide him with hymns. Fanny supplied him with words to "Hold Fast," "Lead Me, My Savior," and "Sunshine on the Hill." As before, many of her hymns were paraphrases of her earlier works.

Fanny worked with a number of other younger musicians as well. Adam Geibel, who was born in Germany, had also become blind as an infant from an inept eye treatment. Mary Upham, a distant cousin of Fanny, had had a successful career as a secular concert singer, then decided to quit for religious reasons. Another young man born in Germany, Victor Benke, was the organist at the Bowery Mission.

The person Fanny perhaps liked to work with best was Ira Allan Sankey, the third and youngest son of her good friend Ira Sankey. Young Sankey had been born in Edinburgh, Scotland, in 1874, during his father's first overseas campaign. From an early age, he had shown a love for the arts and especially for music. In time Sankey went to work for Biglow and Main.

Fanny had known Sankey from the time he was a baby and had followed his progress as a composer with much interest. She considered his music "unusually sweet and beautiful." And, as highly regarded as the elder Sankey was in Fanny's eyes, she believed that "the son surpassed the father in sweetness of tone and harmony of expression."

The two began their collaborations in 1899 and continued until Fanny's death sixteen years later. Allan Sankey, more than any other gospel hymn writer, could express the emotional power of Fanny's poems. Some of the more complicated hymns for which he composed music included "God's Peace I'll Know." These tunes were more beautiful to listen to than the ones by Doane and Lowry; they were also more difficult to sing and to play on the organ or piano.

The most popular hymn the two wrote lyrics and music for was "Never Give Up." Allan composed the melody in a simple, straightforward style. Some of the lyrics:

> Never be sad or desponding,
> If thou hath faith to believe,
> Grace, for the duties before thee
> Ask of thy God and receive.
> Never give up, never give up,
> Never give up to thy sorrows;
> Jesus will bid them depart.
> Trust in the Lord, trust in the Lord,
> Sing when your trials are greatest,
> Trust in the Lord and take heart!

Fanny thought the hymn one of her most effective. And it became quite successful, being sung in the 1900s at evangelistic campaigns conducted by evangelist Rodney "Gipsy" Smith (1860–1947).

Also a vice-president of the Leeds and Catlin Phonograph Company, Allan Sankey persuaded some of the outstanding personalities of the Moody-Sankey years to record their voices for posterity. His father made a recording with the remains of his once-beautiful voice, singing "The Ninety and Nine" and some other hymns. Even Moody was persuaded to make one recording in which he recited the Beatitudes. Stebbins, Sam Hadley, and several others were recorded singing hymns. Fanny most likely did not choose to make a recording, because none exists.

Fanny received another blow when her good friend D. L. Moody had to leave his November 1899 campaign in Kansas City due to a heart condition. He was taken by train to Northfield, where he lingered for a month, dying on December 22 at the age of sixty-two.

Sometime later in Brooklyn, a reporter asked Fanny what manner of man D. L. Moody was, and she answered, "I have never known a kinder, bigger-hearted man than Dwight L. Moody. His work was a miracle and a constant inspiration through all my work. His influence was the light—sanative and bracing."

None of her friends' deaths seemed to slow Fanny down, though, as she maintained a rigorous schedule of writing hymns, traveling, preaching, and working in the missions. In the spring, however, shortly after her eightieth birthday, she collapsed from bronchial pneumonia. For the second time in four years, as she said, she was "almost in sight of the harbor." Once more her amazing constitution caused her to rally despite a chronic heart condition.

Fanny's sisters, however, hurried to Brooklyn and to her room on Lafayette Avenue when they found out about her illness and subsequent collapse. The sisters insisted she come with them. Fanny objected, of course, citing numerous reasons why she couldn't come. When they reassured her that she could return to New York for frequent visits, Fanny gave in and returned home with them. So for the first time in sixty-five years, since she was fifteen, Fanny made her home with relatives. She would stay with them for the next six years.

Fanny's good friend Ira Sankey paid the rent and also sent Fanny's sister Carrie money each month to supply any other needs Fanny had. Sankey knew better than to send the money to Fanny, who would turn around and give it away. Her sisters' residence was probably the finest Fanny had ever known. In a good location, the apartment had five large rooms and was a pleasant, comfortable place. Fanny especially enjoyed sitting near a huge bay window in a rocking chair.

Her sister Carrie Rider could be disarmingly frank, but she was also sincere and open. She disliked pretense and deceit. Quiet and painfully shy in public, Carrie put up with the aggravations of public life for Fanny's sake. Carrie devoted the rest of her life to being her sister's eyes. With gratitude, Fanny said of her later, "She has sacrificed her life for me."

Carrie also became Fanny's secretary. She would read all the mail addressed to Fanny, then respond to it with Fanny's dictated replies. Further, each morning Carrie would write down any poem or hymn "Sister Fan" had composed during the night. Carrie actually performed the duties of two or three secretaries at Biglow and Main.

Carrie's church membership was at the First Baptist Church in Bridgeport, and Fanny sometimes joined her there. But more often she liked to go with Jule to the First Methodist Church. Fanny did not transfer her membership for a few years, but from the first she became active in the King's Daughters, a charitable organization connected with the church, which operated a hospital and supplied food, clothes, and coal for the poor.

Fanny also got involved in Bridgeport's Christian Union, an institution that served the same purpose as New York's rescue missions. Each night a service was held for as many derelicts and drunkards as could be rounded up for an audience. On the nights when Fanny was in town, she would be the main speaker.

The month of August always took Fanny back to Northfield, but now it was a sadder, quieter place with Moody gone. She stayed with the Sankeys in their summer home and visited with Moody's widow, Emma. She also spoke at the Northfield conference, Sankey leading her to the podium. At the end of the conference, she went on to Tully Lake in her role as poet laureate.

Though she lived in Bridgeport, Fanny continued to supply Allan Sankey and Hugh Main with hymns, which were now published in collections of six, seven, and eight instead of in large hymnals. William Howard Doane, however, was preparing a new full-length hymnal that he planned to title *Songs of Devotion*, and he asked Fanny to help him. Fanny went to his summer home at Watch Hill, Rhode Island, and spent several weeks.

While Fanny was there, she received word that her husband, Van, had died. She had continued to visit him, and the two had maintained an amiable relationship. He had been ill with cancer for more than a year and then had suffered a paralytic stroke.

Fanny took Van's death hard. She remembered the June day half a century before when the "voice of love" had first spoken to them both and "all the world was changed." Though they had not been together in a long time, in their own way they had loved each other to the end.

18

Strength at Eighty

C arrie had all she could do to keep up with her sister Fanny, who was gone almost as much as she was home. The days she was at home, she hosted a kind of "open house," which meant that anyone could come and visit with her or receive counsel. When there were no visitors, she worked with the King's Daughters and at the Christian Union. Even in her eighties, Fanny was not one to sit around and rest. Resting was for old people, and she was young, she said.

Fanny had one of the most gratifying experiences of her life in November 1903. She was speaking in Lynn, Massachusetts, at the YMCA, recounting stories of how she came to write certain hymns. This time she spoke about "Rescue the Perishing," saying that it was inspired by the conversion of a young workingman who rejoiced that "Now I can meet my mother in heaven, for now I have found her God!"

At the close of the meeting, a number of people came forward to shake Fanny's hand. Among them was a man whose voice trembled more than his hand. Fanny was stunned when he announced, "Miss Crosby, I was that boy who told you more than thirty-five years ago that he had wandered from his mother's God. That evening you spoke, I sought and found peace, and I have tried to live a consistent Christian life ever since. If we never meet again on earth, we will meet up yonder." He left without giving his name, but Fanny was deeply moved by this "friend who touched a deep chord of sympathy in my heart."

In January 1904 Fanny left by train on a grueling speaking tour, accompanied by her niece, Ida Leschon. They traveled first to Philadelphia, where Fanny held a series of evangelical meetings. Then they went north to Albany, New York, and afterward to Rochester. Fanny had become a national celebrity and was at the highest point of her fame. A Rochester newspaper noted that scarcely a religious service was held in the United States in which one of her hymns was not sung.

Those who saw Fanny at this time took note of her youthful manner. Even though her face and physique may have betrayed her age, her voice, mind, and carriage reflected a woman in her prime. Reporters maintained that "Madame Crosby" could pass for a woman twenty years younger.

Early in February Fanny and Ida went to New York again for the forty-year celebration of Fanny's employment with Biglow and Main. Many of Fanny's old friends were present at the banquet including Doane, the jolly "professor" Kirkpatrick, and George Stebbins. They had all come to honor the poet who more than anyone else had helped make Biglow and Main one of the leading publishers of church music in the English-speaking world. Fanny was presented with a lovely gold brooch embedded with pearls for her special part in the company's success.

Before returning to Bridgeport, Fanny called on Ira Sankey, who had become blind. Sankey had suffered much depression over the loss of his sight, which was the result of glaucoma. Fanny was devastated when she learned of Sankey's state and sought to cheer him up with her visit. But Sankey had given in to his condition; he no longer wrote tunes or appeared in public. Instead, he spent his days sitting in his bedroom lost in memories or playing over and over on his harmonium the tunes of happier days.

In June Fanny and Carrie went to Buffalo, New York, where Fanny was the major speaker at a Christian Endeavor convention. Despite her age, she spoke three times each day, often to crowds of more than three thousand. She not only delivered sermons, but also lectured on missions work and the methods of hymn writing.

In all of Fanny's appearances in Buffalo, she moved her hearers, but on one special night she joined the soloist who was singing "Saved by Grace." Scheduled to speak when he finished, she sat behind him on the platform. When the baritone named Jacobs reached the third stanza, Fanny leaped to her feet and began to sing, "Someday, when fades the golden sun. Beneath the rosy-tinted west. . . ." At first her voice seemed "quavering and faltering," as one might expect of an eighty-four-year-old, and Jacobs lowered his strong voice so that Fanny's might be heard. Her voice, however, became higher and stronger as the chorus continued: "And I shall see Him face to face. . . ." The notes filled the hall, and the audience sat enraptured by the beauty and pathos of the moment. Not only did Fanny's audiences appreciate her prepared talks and messages, her spontaneous acts such as this one endeared her to her fans.

Leaving Buffalo, Fanny went on to Binghamton, stopping at various places en route. People were amazed at her vitality. Even Carrie, who was twenty years younger, remarked, "She can tire out everyone present, then go home fresh!" Fanny believed that if she kept busy she would always remain young. If she stopped working, she doubted she would last another year.

Fanny always enjoyed Christmas. Every year after the family dinner, she would compose humorous poems on the spot. While the children rested, she made little gifts to be put in the grab bag for later in the evening, and the humorous poems were copied and given out to each family member.

One of Fanny's delights at these times was playing with the children. One time her grandnephew, Ralph Booth, begged her to go for a ride on his sled. And to the absolute amazement of his parents, Aunt Fanny seated herself on the sled and let Ralph pull her around the backyard in the snow.

The first part of 1905, Fanny and Ida traveled to western New York, where Fanny spoke to a mass meeting of the Railroad YMCA. The next stop was the YMCA's Women's Auxiliary in Rochester. Fanny spoke to the women and also received a tribute. After this, she was expected in Albany, to speak to the Railroad YMCA there.

On March 24, 1905, Fanny would be eighty-five years old. A group of New York ministers, encouraged by Hugh Main and Allan Sankey, decided to hold a Fanny Crosby Sunday on March 26. The celebration was widely publicized to churches all over the country. Dr. Louis Klopsch, editor of the well-respected *Christian Herald*, recommended that all churches honor Fanny Crosby on the selected Sunday. It was also suggested that her hymns be used exclusively in the services and a "love offering" be taken for the beloved hymn writer.

Never one to be swayed by people's ideas, Fanny did not get overly excited when she learned of the special day. She did not try to stop it, but she did express concern that God receive the glory and not her.

Fanny Crosby Day was observed not only in America

but also in England and in such unlikely countries as India and Tasmania. Fanny received many tributes, including letters from people she had never met and from places she had never visited. Former president Grover Cleveland commended her "continuous and disinterested labor in uplifting humanity and pointing out the way to an appreciation of God's goodness and mercy."

Hugh Main had given Fanny a reception a few days prior to the festivities. On her birthday, she went to a reception at the First Methodist Church in Bridgeport looking like a "fragile flower." The ushers led her to a special pew draped with an American flag. Fanny had a dreadful headache but carried on bravely. She spoke briefly of her God, "the sunshine of my soul," and thanked her audience warmly for their love. The choir sang a hymn she had written for the occasion: "O Land of Joy Unseen," put to music by Fred King, one of the parishioners.

On Sunday Fanny gave the evening message at the First Baptist Church, where her sister Carrie attended. The crowd was so large it overflowed the sanctuary into the Sunday school rooms.

At the close of all the festivities throughout the country, Fanny received several thousand dollars in love offerings. This time she accepted the monetary gift. She was overcome by the outward display of the nation's love for her, and her heart was full as she rejoiced in it.

19

Meaningful Times

I n the fall of 1905 Fanny traveled throughout Massachusetts and New Jersey giving lectures. While at home, however, she continued to work on her autobiography. She had started it several years earlier when numerous people had urged her to write her story.

Internationally known, Fanny had lived a long and interesting life. Many people had written partial accounts of her history, appearing in various newspapers and journals. Dr. Robert Lowry had written a brief sketch of her life as an introduction to *Bells at Evening*, and two or three years later Will Carleton's articles about Fanny came out in his *Every Where* magazine. Fanny was so unassuming that she could not understand why anyone would want to know about her. But once her friends convinced her that the public had a genuine interest in her life, she sent her friend Adelbert White to the New York Institution for the Blind to retrieve information about her years there.

Complications quickly developed, however, as Carleton told Fanny of his desire to organize his articles about her into book form. He offered her the same royalty he received from a publisher for his own books on poetry. Fanny said she was not at all concerned about the royalties and gave him permission to organize the biography. Even though she preferred to do her own, she hesitated to deny Carleton permission to do what he wished with his articles.

Then Adelbert White and the personnel at Biglow and Main got involved. They, too, had an interest in Fanny's biography. They still harbored somewhat of a grudge against Carleton for having allegedly worked at cross-purposes with their *Bells at Evening* publication by publishing his articles in his own magazine *Every Where*.

Things went from bad to worse as several factions wrangled over Fanny's biography. Adelbert and Carrie, in particular, were concerned about the future of the autobiography that Fanny was still in the process of compiling. Fanny tried to stay out of everyone's way, but she did feel that the stories that had already been published about her life left out many aspects of it. Fanny also suffered embarrassment over the implication by Phoebe Knapp and others that she lived in poverty due to the unfair wages of her employers. She quickly proclaimed that it was her own choice to live the way she had. She was almost ashamed to live in such luxury as she did now in her sister's home in Bridgeport.

The entire matter came to an abrupt halt when Carleton's wife died suddenly, and he came to realize that he had embarrassed Fanny. Nevertheless, Fanny got her story written under the title *Memories of Eighty Years*. The fact that parts of the book were written hastily makes it compare somewhat unfavorably with Carleton's original articles, in which Fanny had participated at a more relaxed pace.

With the various biographies selling to an interested public, the donations she received from various lectures, and the love offerings from Fanny Crosby Day, Fanny's overall status changed abruptly from being near poverty to something resembling affluence. Embarrassed at first by this turn of events, Fanny soon realized that now she had more money to give to the poor.

Not long after the publication of *Memories of Eighty Years*, Fanny became concerned for Carrie. In the summer of 1906 Carrie developed intestinal cancer. She failed gradually, to the point where she could neither care for herself or for Fanny. Soon both women moved in with their niece Florence Booth. The Booths lived with their two nearly grown children in a big house on Wells Street. The following June, Carrie died at the age of sixty-three. As with every other circumstance in her life, Fanny accepted Carrie's death, saying, "Well, it is God's will, and she is much happier."

Fanny would spend the rest of her life with the Booths. Her niece Florence and another woman, Eva Cleaveland, took dictation and handled her business affairs. Eva went to Fanny's home daily to handle correspondence and write down all the hymns and poems she composed. Although Fanny traveled less now, she did not get much rest. Visitors of all kinds besieged her, including journalists who made her the subject of numerous newspaper and magazine articles. Nearly every day at home there were so many who wanted to see Fanny, they had to make appointments with Eva Cleaveland. People came from all walks of life and for various reasons. Some asked advice about educating or rehabilitating a blind child; Fanny found those questions the most difficult. Others sought her guidance in writing poetry; she had opportunities to coach those with poetic ability, although the majority had little or none. Then there were those who simply wanted her autograph, and others who were unscrupulous—taking an article of her clothing or a piece of jewelry to keep as souvenirs.

Though physically little more than a skeleton, Fanny possessed a beautiful spirit. In addition, people spoke of the sweetness and beauty of her voice. Her speech patterns were typical of a rural New Englander, her vowel endings sounding like "er" as in "Longfeller," a favorite poet.

For someone so small, Fanny was a hearty eater, but she began to require more sleep. After arising each morning about eleven, she would have her coffee, and then eat a large dinner. She was careful what she ate, eating very little meat but good quantities of eggs, fruit, and vegetables.

Fanny was neat in her dress and particular about the wig she wore in her later years. To keep up with the news, she always asked someone to read one of the New York papers to her in the morning.

Fanny's day generally ended around midnight. In the evening hours she would dictate replies to correspondence and then retire to her room. There she prayed and wrote hymns for several hours. If she couldn't sleep, she would spend the time praying for those who had poured their hearts out to her during the day.

The first thing people focused on when they met Fanny was her blindness. But she regarded her affliction as a gift from God, saying, "It was the best thing that could have happened to me" and "How in the world could I have lived such a helpful life as I have lived had I not been blind?" She believed that without her blindness she would never have received an education. Further, if she had not gone to the Institution for the Blind in New York, she would not have had the contacts to allow her to write hymns for a nationally known publishing firm.

Fanny also thought that sight must be a distraction. She had been able to develop her memory and powers of concentration because of her blindness. She sensed, too, that her lack of sight enhanced her appeal as a speaker, creating a bond of sympathy between her and her audiences that made them receptive to the Gospel message.

Her acute hearing made her sensitive to any discord or disharmony. On one occasion, a man who needed to get her attention walked past her hotel room whistling off-key, whereupon Fanny awoke with a start.

Many people still wondered if she harbored any bitterness toward the man who caused her blindness. Again, she was quick to say, "Don't blame the doctor. He is probably dead before this time. But if I could meet him, I would tell him that he unwittingly did me the greatest favor in the world." Moreover, she had doubts as to whether any medical treatment could have saved her defective eyes.

Fanny sensed that her lack of physical sight enabled her to have a keener "soul-vision." She believed she could see into the spiritual world. With unusual perception, Fanny was often aware of the state of the souls of persons with whom she dealt. She could sense who was sincere, who was phony, who was malevolent, and who was kind.

Her spiritual counsel was so helpful and encouraging that many people asked her to write about her theology. She would tell them, however, that "I have never thought much about theology." Fanny had little interest in theology as an academic discipline. She believed spiritual wisdom came not so much from the mind as from the heart and soul and from fellowship with Christ. When faced with a decision, she would ask, "Is this from God?" rather than "Is this rational?" or "Is this logical?"

Her simple convictions helped her transcend the bounds of denominationalism. Whatever church people belonged to, they were all Fanny's "brothers" and "sisters" if they believed in Jesus Christ as revealed by Scripture. She lived into the era when biblical critics began to analyze the Scriptures according to human reason. This practice greatly disturbed her: she believed the Bible was the authoritative Word of God and that it was inspired by the Holy Spirit.

For her, the real essence of Christianity was what the Scriptures and sacraments pointed to: a genuine and personal relationship with God. Fanny went to Him with all her needs, whether large or small. And she knew God faithfully answered prayer.

She also accepted evil as part of life; she believed in a real Satan and that the evil in the world is real. Although God does not "order" it, Fanny would say, He permits evil at times in order to bring good out of it. She would cite her own blindness as a prime example.

Fanny trusted the Lord at all times, and could be extremely cheerful, even in suffering. She knew God always had a good reason for allowing affliction. To illustrate, she would quote Hebrews 12:6, saying, " 'Whom the Lord loveth he chasteneth.' " She would later comment, "If I had no troubles, I'd think the Lord didn't love me!"

Some people thought Fanny's cheerful disposition in her later years came from a naturally happy one. But earlier in her life, she had gone through some terrible times of depression and discouragement. She admitted that her life had been short of many things that some people would rather have died than been without. Yes, she had suffered. But she could look back and see how God had brought much good from it, and she chose to rejoice.

When she was asked why some of her happiest hymns were about death, Fanny would reply, "Since my childhood, death has seemed to me simply a stepping-stone to something better. Why should I be sad about that? I have had moments when it almost seemed I had reached heaven. Could I possibly be less happy when I reach home for good?"

Fanny's joy was not simply a calm and holy serenity, but often outright hilarity. She was considered a very humorous person. As a girl, Fanny enjoyed playing practical jokes, and in old age she tended to be mischievous. Her lectures and sermons were riddled with humorous stories. She sensed the best way to chide or criticize was by making people laugh at their own weaknesses. She could also turn her humor into a barb when she wanted to. She met a reserved, pompous bishop one night at Phoebe Knapp's and was turned off by his solemnity. When the man excused himself to leave, Fanny called out in the presence of the other guests: "For heaven's sake, Bishop, stay sober!"

By the time Fanny had reached her eighties, she was known as "the Methodist saint." In fact, many who knew her had an even higher estimate of her, considering her "the most wonderful person living"—an amazing tribute indeed.

20

Changing Times

Rain or shine, snow or cold, Fanny stayed on the move—and this would continue, even past the age of ninety. More and more, though, in the winter of 1907–1908, she stayed indoors, greeting the many visitors who came to see her. She wrote to Adelbert White at the time, "I am staying indoors until the weather shall moderate." By March, however, she got on the train at Bridgeport and journeyed alone to New York City, where her good friend Phoebe Knapp met her, and with whom she spent the week.

Just in time for her annual March banquet, Fanny was asked about her many hymns. Which hymn did she consider the best one? Without hesitation she declared, "I have not yet written my best hymn."

Fanny knew that many of her hymns had been used by God to benefit many people and to point them to Him, but she sensed that from an artistic point of view, she had not written many great ones. Because she often felt rushed in writing hymns, she lacked the time to refine them. Maybe from now on she could take more time to compose her poems in a painstaking way and revise them as necessary.

Fanny spent the week following her birthday at a

Methodist convention in Brooklyn. On a free afternoon she went to see Ira Sankey for what would be the last time. He had lingered for three years with a debilitating illness that caused him great pain and took him down physically to a shadow of his former self. Fanny regarded Sankey with compassion, telling him, "The entire Christian world is praying for your recovery." But he just shook his head, and said, "I'll meet you in heaven—at the pearly gate at the eastern side of the city." Then the great singer added, "There, I'll take you by the hand and lead you along the golden street, up to the throne of God, and there we'll stand and say to Him, 'And now we see Thee face to face, saved by Thy matchless, boundless grace!'" As she left his room, Fanny sensed it would be the last time she would see Sankey on earth.

But she had much work to do, and after leaving the convention, Fanny traveled to Perth Amboy, New Jersey, for a two-week speaking engagement. There, she also said good-bye to Phoebe Knapp at the Hotel Savoy—not knowing it would be the last time she would see Phoebe.

Now Fanny went on to Princeton, where she addressed the congregation at a sacred concert on Good Friday at the Presbyterian church. On Sunday morning she preached the Easter sermon.

She visited her old friend Grover Cleveland before leaving Princeton. At the time of her visit, Cleveland was feeble and emaciated, and Fanny was much concerned for him. She needed to continue her journey, however, and traveled on to New Haven to see Adelbert White at Yale. Sometime later, on June 25, Fanny learned that Cleveland had died. She was comforted by their "deep, warm friendship that death cannot break, for the cords will be united and we shall see and know each other in the land of the blest."

A scant two weeks after Fanny learned of Cleveland's death, she received word that Phoebe had died suddenly. In her seventies, Phoebe had remained vigorous and youthful. She had been vacationing in Maine, when she suffered a fatal stroke.

Only a month later Ira Sankey died. On the morning of August 13 he had passed into a coma as he sang the opening lines of Fanny's "Saved by Grace":

> Someday the silver cord will break
> And I no more as now shall sing,
> But, oh, the joy when I shall wake
> Within the palace of the King!

That evening, Sankey breathed his last breath.

Fanny could have felt lonely and bereft of the many good friends of her generation whom she had outlived, as well as some of the younger generation. But Fanny possessed an indomitable spirit and confessed that she was "as happy as a chickadee." She rested secure in the confidence that she would see her loved ones again, and she had assurance that God even now had a purpose for her on earth.

She still wrote hymns, mostly for Allan Sankey and Charles Gabriel, plus a few for Hugh Main. She composed a successful hymn on the transitory nature of earthly life called "We're Traveling On," which represented the last of her major hymns. During this time she continued to speak regularly at the Christian Union, and she kept up her ministry of encouragement through private meetings, letters, lectures, and hospital visitations.

Many changes had occurred throughout Fanny's long lifetime. She had witnessed the invention of the telephone, the telegraph, the steam engine, the phonograph, the moving picture, the bicycle, the typewriter, the X-ray, the elevator, the sewing machine, the safety

match, anesthetics, the reaper and the mower, the sub-
marine, the typesetting machine, the automobile, the
airplane, and the radio. She even developed some appreciation for the "new" modern poetry that lacked
rhyme and rhythm. To some extent, she also enjoyed the
popular songs of the day, but felt that she could "elevate
them above their present standard."

From the time the stories of her life began circulat-
ing, Fanny had been affectionately known as "Aunt
Fanny," considered almost an American patron saint.
Now she became concerned about various trends she
saw developing in American society. One of them was
the erosion of the American home and family structure.
Fanny disagreed with the aims of the fledgling women's
movement; she grumbled that modern women seemed
eager to do everything but "the work that ought to be
done at home." She remarked further that "I may appear a little old-fogeyish, but I have firm convictions on
this very vital question." She believed that the nation's
strength lay in family and homelife. If these remained
strong, the nation would, too.

She had a firm conviction as well that God should be
at the center of the home. She expressed great concern
as she saw the waning interest in Christianity among
Americans. Speaking of the Bible, she noted, "When I
was a child, this book had a practical place both in the
home and the nation." She felt sad about the growing
doubts and disbelief of Scripture, remarking, "No Christian nation can be great that ignores the Sacred Book."
Moreover, America would not last "if the heads of the
families are prayerless."

The nation, too, Aunt Fanny maintained, must be
headed by a man of prayer. She made these remarks
while William Howard Taft, a nominal Unitarian, was
in the White House. Fanny said the nation could not
survive with "prayerless Presidents." In fact, without a

return to the faith of their fathers, America did not have a future.

As change swirled around her, Fanny continued doing the things she had always done. She realized that church attendance had decreased and that fewer and fewer men seemed "interested in religion." She was concerned that from the generation rising about her "there will not be men enough in heaven to sing bass."

The structure of Protestantism itself was undergoing change. Numerous modern theologians had come to question the authority of Scripture—especially with the rise of German "Higher Criticism," which attributed the Bible to human authors. No longer was the Bible considered the inspired Word of God with the Holy Spirit as its Divine Author.

Not all the developments within Protestantism troubled her. She observed with much interest the career of Reverend W. A. (Billy) Sunday, who in many ways proved to be D. L. Moody's successor. Other people who gave Fanny hope for the future and inspired her were Dr. J. Wilbur Chapman and his "chorister" Charles M. Alexander, who conducted a successful multinational campaign in 1909. Aunt Fanny even honored them with a poem.

Fanny's ninetieth birthday came in March 1910. Although her body was bent nearly in two, she continued to travel and lecture. She refused to quit and give in to the ravages of time. A letter to Bert White shows her state of mind: "I am so busy I hardly know my name." If anything, her cheerfulness increased more and more rather than diminish because of age. She told people, "I don't want to die yet, but rather live on for another decade-and-a-half, to the age of one hundred and five." She was quick to add, however, that if her heavenly Father willed otherwise, "It is well." She attributed her longevity to "angel-guards" who controlled her appetite, temper, and speech.

Once more, in the spring of 1911, Fanny took the train alone to New York City. She appeared as the main speaker at the "Tent, Open-Air, and Shop Campaign" of the Evangelistic Committee of the Methodist Episcopal Church. The meeting took place at Carnegie Hall with over five thousand people present; a choir of two thousand sang many of Fanny's best-known hymns.

Fanny arrived there in an automobile and in somewhat of a flurry. When the car pulled up, the doormen were so astonished at her wasted appearance that one of them shouted, "For heaven's sake, get a wheelchair!"

But Fanny's strong voice boomed forth, "*I* need no rolling chair. I can stand on my own two feet. My strength is in the Lord."

That October Fanny went back to New York for the last time to visit Helen Keller, whom she had met ten years before. She spent a day with the woman whom she regarded as a modern prophet. Following their visit, she spoke at the Bowery Mission. Then she traveled to Jersey City and spoke at the Simpson Memorial Methodist Church. There she also saw an old friend from her Institution days, Alice Holmes. The two women had not been together for four decades, but Alice recognized Fanny at once by her voice.

Soon afterward, everyone thought Aunt Fanny had reached the end when she was stricken with pneumonia. To their amazement—even her own—she rallied. Only now she looked so frail everyone expected her to go at anytime.

But Fanny continued to travel occasionally, and in February 1913 she and Florence Booth went to Cambridge, Massachusetts, so Fanny could speak at the First Baptist Church. She preached to an audience of two thousand at one service. Several years later a man who had attended the service as a child recalled "the little old lady, dressed in black, standing with Dr. Campbell behind the lectern, saying good-bye to the world."

When she reached the age of ninety-three at Easter 1913, Fanny remarked, "If there is anyone in this world happier than I, I want to shake his hand, for I believe myself to be as happy as it is possible for a mortal to be in this world. Life with me glides on like a little boat on a waveless stream with flowers on each bank."

In the evening she attended the First Methodist Church. George Stebbins came from Brooklyn to be with her; he was accompanied by his neighbor Mrs. Jenny Bennett Carpenter, a blind soprano. In New York, a few years earlier, Fanny had heard Mrs. Bennett sing and was impressed with her ability. After Fanny finished speaking that night, Jenny sang "Saved by Grace." Halfway through the hymn, Aunt Fanny got up, took the woman's arm, and sang with her. A wave of emotion surged through the congregation as the two blind women stood singing together in a never-to-be-forgotten moment.

As Fanny wrote to Bert White, most of her time from then on was spent knitting, stopping when callers came or something more pressing presented itself. She enjoyed occasional automobile rides and seeing a few friends, but other than those activities, she seldom traveled anymore. As her ninety-fourth birthday approached, the King's Daughters decreed that all Fanny's friends should wear her favorite flower, the violet, to honor her. Further, Hugh Main got in touch with the newspapers telling them about "Violet Day" so it could be publicized.

The Sunday prior to the special day, Fanny spoke at First Methodist Church for what was to be the last time. The sanctuary was full, and a local newspaper reported that she was "feeble in body, yet strong in mind; buoyant in spirit, with a trust and faith in God as firm as the everlasting hills."

Much of what she said that day was about the power of prayer. She told the people that prayer is essential in a believer's life. She also asserted that a person need not kneel or assume a particular position to pray. She told them that "I do not kneel to pray. I no longer have the strength to rise from that position." Then she added that believers should feel free to pray on all occasions and in whatever position.

In conclusion, she shared several examples of God's answering prayer, including her own recovery from pneumonia, which she attributed to the prayers of her friends. Again, she stressed that "I want all of you to go to God in prayer in all trials and sorrows. The good will come out of it, and He will answer your prayer better than you think." Of course, a person may not always get exactly what he requests, but one must trust God's way as best. Then she urged the people to "cling to the Savior" in "this age of change." Finally, she said, "My dear, dear people, I love you dearly, and if I should first cross to that beautiful shore, I know that I shall greet you there!" However, never feeling her work was quite finished, she would always say, "I believe that He still has work for me; I don't want to die yet."

It did seem, however, to those who were closest to Fanny, that the day might not be far off. Perhaps she would not attain her wished-for goal of 105 years.

21

Twilight Hours

As was customary, Fanny and Jule spent the last day of May celebrating their mother Mercy's birthday at Jule's home. Death was much on the mind of each of the old women, and Fanny sensed about Carrie, "I know that she is very near me." Fanny spoke often in those days of loved ones that had gone on before her and how she longed to see them again.

A mild heart attack in August 1914 laid Aunt Fanny low. Again, it seemed her time had come. During the illness, she experienced some ecstatic visions, and upon recovery she claimed they were the most remarkable she had ever had. She did not elaborate on them, except to say that an angel came to her in one, telling her, "Be thou faithful, and I will give thee the crown of life"—almost word for word from the book of Revelation. The angel added, "Be calm and get your strength back as soon as you can, and then go to work for the Master once more."

That was all Fanny needed to rally once more, and she did partially recover. But the doctors told her niece Florence that she could not live much longer. Fanny was joyful about her approaching end. She thought death would be to "pass on to the glorious land," and she said to her friends, "When I have arrived at my eternal home, they will say, 'Come in, Fanny! Come in!' Then will be the victory through Christ!"

As the angel had commanded her, however, while life lasted, she still had "work for the Master." First of all, Fanny thought the angel wanted her to give the world a few more hymns before she departed. To accommodate her, Allan Sankey and Hugh Main were collaborating on their first major hymnal in a decade and asked Fanny to contribute. Over the next months, Fanny wrote about a dozen hymns. Among the best was "Keep Thou Me."

Fanny heard from Doane in January; he suffered from "creeping paralysis" and was bedridden. He could sit up only a few minutes each day, but he had decided to write one final song. In a letter, he asked Fanny to write the lyrics. In early February Fanny wrote her last hymn:

> At evening time it shall be light,
> When fades the day of toil away,
> No shadows deep, no weary night,
> At evening time, it shall be light.
> At evening time it shall be light,
> Immortal love from realms above
> Is breathing now the promise bright,
> At evening time it shall be light.

From then on Fanny's thoughts were taken up with her own death and burial. She insisted, first of all, that Florence and Jule not have any marble or granite memorial erected—such as P. T. Barnum had had erected to himself. Instead, she requested something that would benefit people. Some of the suggestions she gave them were the Christian Union's need for an infirmary, or perhaps a home for elderly people. She knew of various individuals who had little companionship when they got old, and she thought a way could be found to alleviate their situations. She suggested, too, a fund to help elderly ministers, for whom there was no pension at the time. Whatever the two women decided to set up as Fanny's memorial, they were not to erect a monument.

Then Fanny contacted a lawyer to draw up a will. She left half her estate to Florence for her care over the years; the rest was to be put in a trust for Jule. When Jule should die, her share would go to Florence.

On February 8 a group of mission workers visited Fanny. As she spoke to them about her life, she shared her concern for four categories of people: railroad men, policemen, prisoners, and the poor. She also told them what she had said to people many times before about her blindness: "The loss of sight has been no loss to me."

During Fanny's final weeks, she manifested a strange phenomenon. Numerous visitors commented that her countenance seemed to visibly shine "full of radiant light." The visible glowing was first apparent on isolated occasions as early as 1907, but it became more or less constant in Fanny's last days. The mission workers witnessed it the day they came, and the next day, February 9, Rev. H. A. Davenport of the People's Presbyterian Church, visited and also noticed the unusual radiance.

On February 10 Adam Geibel came to see Fanny, and the two blind musicians played a piano duet. But the following day Fanny said she felt ill and decided to remain in bed. Further, she did not feel hungry, which was unusual for her. But she announced, "Tomorrow I shall be well," and as she said it she seemed radiant with joy. Throughout the day she kept smiling and saying, "I'm so comfortable. I'm so comfortable."

At nine that evening, Fanny sent for Eva Cleaveland asking her to write a letter of consolation to a neighboring family who had just lost a child. She told them, "Your precious Ruth is safe in the arms of Jesus." Upon completion of the letter, Fanny dictated her final testimony to the world:

> In the morn of Zion's glory,
> When the clouds have rolled away,
> And my hope has dropped its anchor
> In the vale of perfect day,
> When with all the pure and holy
> I shall strike my harp anew,
> With a power no arm can sever,
> Love will hold me fast and true.

The last person to retire that evening was Henry Booth. He went upstairs at 2:30 in the morning, looked in on Aunt Fanny, as he usually did, to see how she was. She was awake, heard him, and smiled, saying gently, "All right, Governor." At 3:30, Florence heard Fanny walking down the hall. She got up to help her and met Fanny at the doorway to her room. There, to her horror, her aunt fainted in her arms.

Florence managed to get her back to bed, then awoke her husband and son and called two doctors. Fanny, however, took little notice of what was going on in the room. Earth appeared to be receding now, "the morn of Zion's glory" breaking in upon her. Florence and Henry were amazed at the peace and serenity on her face.

The first of the doctors came at 4:30, and pronounced her dead of a massive cerebral hemorrhage. Florence let out a scream and burst into tears, crying, "It cannot be! It cannot be!" But Eva Cleaveland admitted in a letter to Bert White, "We have had reason to fear that she might have a long unconscious illness or suffer something that way, so that it is a comfort to have her go like this."

Fanny's funeral was reported to be the largest one ever held in Bridgeport—larger even than that of P. T. Barnum. People lined up for blocks to file by the coffin. In Fanny's right hand was the little silk flag she often carried, and at Jule's request, the words *My Sister* were engraved on the casket.

Many people that Fanny had loved were there including George Stebbins, Allan Sankey, and Hugh Main. Flowers that Fanny loved filled the church, and the choir sang her favorite hymn, Heber's "Faith of Our Fathers." After Reverend Davenport prayed at length, the choir sang "Safe in the Arms of Jesus" and "Saved by Grace."

In his eulogy, Dr. Brown said, "You have come to pay tribute and to crown a friend. There must have been a royal welcome when this queen of sacred song burst the bonds of death and passed into the glories of heaven."

Not long after Fanny's death, many of her associates also died. On Christmas Eve Doane died of pneumonia at eighty-four, and three days later Allan Sankey had a heart attack. He died after major surgery in April 1920. The following year, Kirkpatrick died of a heart attack while writing a hymn. Then Hugh Main retired, and his firm merged with the Hope Publishing Company of Chicago. Main died at eighty-six in October 1925. George Stebbins moved to Catskill, New York, continuing to write music and provide a setting to at least one of Fanny's unused poems. He died in October 1945, four months before his 100th birthday.

In 1920, on the 100th anniversary of Fanny's birth, the Christian Union opened an infirmary in Fanny's memory. Two years later a twenty-eight room mansion was endowed in Bridgeport as the Fanny Crosby Memorial Home for aged men and women.

And, until 1955, nothing marked Fanny Crosby's grave except a tiny marble stone with the words "Aunt Fanny" and the inscription "She hath done what she could." On May 1 of that year, however, a large marble slab was erected on her grave, because Bridgeport citizens decided that the "relatively inconspicuous marker with only vague identification" was not worthy of "The Queen of the Gospel Hymn."

The new inscription concludes with a verse from her famous hymn:

> Blessed assurance, Jesus is mine!
> Oh, what a foretaste of glory divine!
> Heir of salvation, purchase of God,
> Born of His spirit, washed in His blood.

Certainly the new inscription befits this giant of a woman who left an indelible mark in song for Christians everywhere.

A Sampling of Fanny Crosby's Best Loved Hymns

Blessed Assurance

Blessed assurance, Jesus is mine!
Oh, what a foretaste of glory divine!
Heir of salvation, purchase of God,
Born of His Spirit, washed in His blood.

CHORUS
This is my story, this is my song,
Praising my Savior all the day long;
This is my story, this is my song,
Praising my Savior all the day long.

Perfect submission, perfect delight,
Visions of rapture now burst on my sight;
Angels descending, bring from above
Echoes of mercy, whispers of love.

Perfect submission, all is at rest,
I in my Savior am happy and blest;
Watching and waiting, looking above,
Filled with His goodness, lost in His love.

Pass Me Not

Pass me not, O gentle Savior,
Hear my humble cry;
While on others Thou art calling,
Do not pass me by.

CHORUS
Savior, Savior, Hear my humble cry;
While on others Thou art calling,
Do not pass me by.

Let me at a throne of mercy
Find a sweet relief;
Kneeling there in deep contrition,
Help my unbelief.

Trusting only in Thy merit,
Would I seek Thy Face;
Heal my wounded, broken spirit,
Save me by Thy grace.

Thou the Spring of all my comfort,
More than life to me,
Whom have I on earth beside Thee?
Whom in Heav'n but Thee?

To God Be the Glory

To God be the glory, great things He hath done,
So loved He the world that He gave us His Son,
Who yielded His life an atonement for sin,
And opened the Lifegate that all may go in.

CHORUS
Praise the Lord, praise the Lord,
Let the earth hear His voice!
Praise the Lord, praise the Lord,
Let the people rejoice!
O come to the Father thro' Jesus the Son,

And give Him the glory,
great things He hath done.

O perfect redemption, the purchase of blood,
To ev'ry believer the promise of God;
The vilest offender who truly believes,
That moment from Jesus a pardon receives.

Great things He hath taught us,
great things He hath done,
And great our rejoicing thro' Jesus the Son;
But purer, and higher, and greater will be
Our wonder, our transport, when Jesus we see.

All the Way My Savior Leads Me

All the way my Savior leads me;
What have I to ask beside?
Can I doubt His tender mercy,
Who through life has been my Guide?
Heavenly peace, divinest comfort,
Here by faith in Him to dwell!
For I know, whate'er befall me,
Jesus doeth all things well.

All the way my Savior leads me,
Cheers each winding path I tread,
Gives me grace for every trial,
Feeds me with the living bread.
Though my weary steps may falter,
And my soul athirst may be,
Gushing from the Rock before me,
Lo! a spring of joy I see.

All the way my Savior leads me;
Oh, the fullness of His love!
Perfect rest to me is promised
In my Father's house above.
When my spirit, clothed immortal,

Wings its flight to realms of day,
This my song through endless ages:
Jesus led me all the way.

Rescue the Perishing

Rescue the perishing, care for the dying,
Snatch them in pity from sin and the grave;
Weep o'er the erring one, lift up the fallen
Tell them of Jesus the mighty to save.

CHORUS
Rescue the perishing, care for the dying;
Jesus is merciful, Jesus will save.

Though they are slighting Him,
Still He is waiting,
Waiting the penitent child to receive;
Plead with them earnestly,
Plead with them gently,
He will forgive if they only believe.

Down in the human heart,
Crushed by the tempter,
Feelings lie buried that grace can restore;
Touched by a loving heart, wakened by kindness,
Chords that were broken will vibrate once more.

Rescue the perishing, duty demands it;
Strength for thy labor the Lord will provide;
Back to the narrow way patiently win them;
Tell the poor wanderer a Savior has died.

Safe in the Arms of Jesus

Safe in the arms of Jesus,
Safe on His gentle breast,
There by His love o'ershaded,
Sweetly my soul shall rest.

Hark! 'tis the voice of angels,
Borne in a song to me,
Over the fields of glory,
Over the jasper sea.

CHORUS
Safe in the arms of Jesus,
Save on His gentle breast,
There by His love o'ershaded,
Sweetly my soul shall rest.

Safe in the arms of Jesus,
Safe from corroding care,
Safe from the world's temptations,
Sin cannot harm me there.
Free from the blight of sorrow,
Free from my doubts and fears;
Only a few more trials,
Only a few more tears!

Jesus, my heart's dear refuge,
Jesus has died for me;
Firm on the Rock of Ages
Ever my trust shall be.
Here let me wait with patience,
Wait till the night is o'er;
Wait till I see the morning
Break on the golden shore.

I Am Thine, O Lord

I am Thine, O Lord, I have heard Thy voice,
And it told Thy love to me;
But I long to rise in the arms of faith,
And be closer drawn to Thee.

CHORUS
Draw me nearer, nearer blessed Lord,
To the cross where Thou hast died;

Draw ne nearer, nearer, nearer, blessed Lord,
To Thy precious, bleeding side.

Consecrate me now to Thy service, Lord,
By the pow'r of grace divine;
Let my soul look up with a steadfast hope,
And my will be lost in Thine.

Oh, the pure delight of a single hour
That before Thy throne I spend,
When I kneel in prayer, and with Thee, my God,
I commune as friend with friend!

There are depths of love that I cannot know
Till I cross the narrow sea;
There are heights of joy that I may not reach
Till I rest in peace with Thee.

INTRODUCE YOURSELF TO ANOTHER HERO OF THE FAITH.

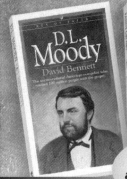

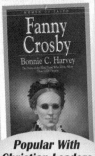

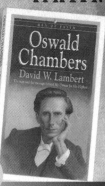

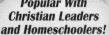

Popular With Christian Leaders and Homeschoolers!

Gathered from across centuries and continents, the biographies in the MEN and WOMEN OF FAITH series all have one thing in common— an inspiring example of a person dedicated to living fully for God. Whether missionary, writer, theologian, or ordinary citizen, each person featured in the series provides us with both encouragement for our own lives as well as an appreciation of our spiritual history.

Often thrilling and always compelling, the MEN and WOMEN OF FAITH biographies ensure that the stories of our Christian heritage will continue to live on.

Thank you for selecting a book from
BETHANY HOUSE PUBLISHERS

Bethany House Publishers is a ministry of Bethany
Fellowship International, an interdenominational,
nonprofit organization committed to spreading the
Good News of Jesus Christ around the world through
evangelism, church planting, literature distribution,
and care for those in need. Missionary training is
offered through Bethany College of Missions.

Bethany Fellowship International is a member of the
National Association of Evangelicals and subscribes to
its statement of faith. If you would like further
information, please contact:

Bethany Fellowship International
6820 Auto Club Road
Minneapolis, MN 55438 USA